The Emotionally Intelligent Leader

The Emotionally Intelligent Leader

DANIEL GOLEMAN

HARVARD BUSINESS REVIEW PRESS
BOSTON, MASSACHUSETTS

Copyright 2019 Harvard Business School Publishing Corporation
Originally published in *Harvard Business Review* in March 2000, January 2004, and December 2013
Reprint #10101, #10102, #R1312B

The web addresses referenced in this book were live and correct at the time of the book's publication but may be subject to change.

Cataloguing-in-Publication data is forthcoming.

ISBN: 978-1-63369-733-1
eISBN: 978-1-63369-734-8

The paper used in this publication meets the requirements of the American National Standard for Permanence of Paper for Publications and Documents in Libraries and Archives Z39.48-1992.

CONTENTS

Preface   vii

What Makes a Leader?   1

The Focused Leader   61

Leadership That Gets Results   113

Index   197

About the Author   209

PREFACE

Best-selling author Daniel Goleman
first brought the concept of emotional
intelligence (EI) to the forefront of business
through his articles in *Harvard Business
Review*, establishing EI as an indispensable
trait for leaders. Three of his most widely
read and respected articles, "What Makes
a Leader?" "The Focused Leader," and
"Leadership That Gets Results," are
presented here, together for the first time.

These three classics show the direct ties between EI, focus, and measurable business results.

In "What Makes a Leader?" Goleman introduces his research that found that truly effective leaders are distinguished by a high degree of EI. The chief components of emotional intelligence—self-awareness, self-regulation, motivation, empathy, and social skill—can be strengthened through persistence, practice, and feedback from colleagues and other leaders. This article shows how to develop the self-management and relationship skills that form the basis of emotionally intelligent leadership.

Learning to focus your attention is increasingly important, as each of us is distracted by technology both at work and at home. In "The Focused Leader," Goleman explains why focus is crucial to great leadership. Every leader needs to cultivate a triad of awareness—an inward focus, a focus on others, and an outward focus. Focusing inward and focusing on others helps leaders cultivate emotional intelligence. Focusing outward can improve their ability to devise strategy, innovate, and manage organizations.

In "Leadership That Gets Results," Goleman explains that many managers mistakenly assume that leadership style is a function of personality rather than strategic choice. Instead of choosing the one style that suits their temperament, leaders should

~~ask which style best addresses the demands of a particular situation.~~ Goleman describes six leadership styles derived from different emotional intelligence competencies—coercive, authoritative, affiliative, democratic, pacesetting, and coaching—and shows how each works best in particular situations and affects the organizational climate in a different way.

Whether you're concerned with developing your own emotional intelligence or recognizing and strengthening EI in others, Goleman's timeless research will prove practical and useful as you become the most effective leader you can be.

What Makes a Leader?

Every businessperson knows a story about a highly intelligent, highly skilled executive who was promoted into a leadership position only to fail at the job. And they also know a story about someone with solid—but not extraordinary—intellectual abilities and technical skills who was promoted into a similar position and then soared.

Such anecdotes support the widespread belief that identifying individuals with the "right stuff" to be leaders is more art than science. After all, the personal styles of superb leaders vary: Some leaders are subdued and analytical; others shout their manifestos from the mountaintops. And just as important, different situations call for different types of leadership. Most mergers need a sensitive negotiator at the helm, whereas many turnarounds require a more forceful authority.

I have found, however, that the most effective leaders are alike in one crucial way: They all have a high degree of what has come to be known as *emotional intelligence*. It's not that IQ and technical skills are irrelevant. They do matter, but mainly as "threshold capabilities"; that is, they are the entry-level requirements for executive positions. But my research, along with other recent studies, clearly shows that emotional intelligence is the sine qua non of leadership. Without it, a person can have the best training in the world, an incisive, analytical mind, and an endless supply of smart ideas, but he still won't make a great leader.

In the course of the past year, my colleagues and I have focused on how emotional intelligence operates at work. We have examined the relationship between emotional intelligence and effective performance, especially in leaders. And we have observed how emotional intelligence shows itself on the job. How can you tell if someone has high emotional intelligence, for example, and how can you recognize it in yourself? In the following pages, we'll explore these questions, taking each of the components of emotional intelligence—self-awareness, self-regulation, motivation, empathy, and social skill—in turn.

EVALUATING EMOTIONAL INTELLIGENCE

Most large companies today have employed trained psychologists to develop what are known as "competency models" to aid them in identifying, training, and promoting likely stars in the leadership firmament. The psychologists have also developed such models for lower-level positions. And in

recent years, I have analyzed competency
models from 188 companies, most of which
were large and global and included the likes
of Lucent Technologies, British Airways,
and Credit Suisse.

In carrying out this work, my objective
was to determine which personal
capabilities drove outstanding performance
within these organizations, and to what
degree they did so. I grouped capabilities
into three categories: purely technical
skills like accounting and business
planning; cognitive abilities like analytical
reasoning; and competencies demonstrating
emotional intelligence, such as the ability
to work with others and effectiveness in
leading change.

To create some of the competency models, psychologists asked senior managers at the companies to identify the capabilities that typified the organization's most outstanding leaders. To create other models, the psychologists used objective criteria, such as a division's profitability, to differentiate the star performers at senior levels within their organizations from the average ones. Those individuals were then extensively interviewed and tested, and their capabilities were compared. This process resulted in the creation of lists of ingredients for highly effective leaders. The lists ranged in length from seven to 15 items and included such ingredients as initiative and strategic vision.

When I analyzed all this data, I found dramatic results. To be sure, intellect was a driver of outstanding performance. Cognitive skills such as big-picture thinking and long-term vision were particularly important. But when I calculated the ratio of technical skills, IQ, and emotional intelligence as ingredients of excellent performance, emotional intelligence proved to be twice as important as the others for jobs at all levels.

Moreover, my analysis showed that emotional intelligence played an increasingly important role at the highest levels of the company, where differences in technical skills are of negligible importance. In other words, the higher the rank of a person considered to be a star performer, the more emotional intelligence capabilities showed up as the reason for his or her effectiveness. When I compared star performers with average ones in senior leadership positions, nearly 90% of the difference in their profiles was attributable to emotional intelligence factors rather than cognitive abilities.

Other researchers have confirmed that emotional intelligence not only distinguishes outstanding leaders but can also be linked to strong performance. The findings of the late David McClelland, the renowned researcher in human and organizational behavior, are a good example. In a 1996 study of a global food and beverage company, McClelland found that when senior managers had a critical mass of emotional intelligence capabilities, their divisions outperformed yearly earnings goals by 20%. Meanwhile, division leaders without that critical mass underperformed by almost the same amount. McClelland's findings, interestingly, held as true in the company's U.S. divisions as in its divisions in Asia and Europe.

In short, the numbers are beginning to tell us a persuasive story about the link between a company's success and the emotional intelligence of its leaders. And just as important, research is also demonstrating that people can, if they take the right approach, develop their emotional intelligence. (See the sidebar "Can Emotional Intelligence Be Learned?")

Can Emotional Intelligence Be Learned?

For ages, people have debated if leaders are born or made. So too goes the debate about emotional intelligence. Are people born with certain levels of empathy, for example, or do they acquire empathy as a result of life's experiences? The answer is both. Scientific inquiry strongly suggests that there is a genetic component to emotional intelligence. Psychological and developmental research indicates that nurture plays a role as well. How much of each perhaps will never be known, but research and practice clearly demonstrate that emotional intelligence can be learned.

One thing is certain: Emotional intelligence increases with age. There is an old-fashioned word for the phenomenon: maturity. Yet even with maturity, some people still need training to enhance their emotional intelligence. Unfortunately, far too many training programs that intend to build leadership skills—including emotional intelligence—are a waste of time and money. The problem is simple: They focus on the wrong part of the brain.

Emotional intelligence is born largely in the neurotransmitters of the brain's limbic system, which governs feelings, impulses, and drives. Research indicates that the limbic system learns best through motivation, extended practice, and feedback. Compare this with the kind of learning that goes on in the neocortex, which governs analytical and technical ability. The neocortex grasps concepts and logic. It is the part of the brain that figures out how to use a computer or make a sales call by reading a book. Not surprisingly—but mistakenly—it is also the part of the brain targeted by most training programs aimed at enhancing emotional intelligence. When such programs take, in effect, a neocortical approach, my research with the Consortium for Research on Emotional Intelligence in Organizations has shown they can even have a *negative* impact on people's job performance.

To enhance emotional intelligence, organizations must refocus their training to include the limbic system. They must help people break old behavioral habits and establish new ones. That not only takes much more time than conventional training programs, it also requires an individualized approach.

Imagine an executive who is thought to be low on empathy by her colleagues. Part of that deficit shows itself as an inability to listen; she interrupts people and doesn't pay close attention to what they're saying. To fix the problem, the executive needs to be motivated to change, and then she needs practice and feedback from others in the company. A colleague or coach could be tapped to let the executive know when she has been observed failing to listen. She would then have to replay the incident and give a better response; that is, demonstrate her ability to absorb what others are saying. And the executive could be directed to observe certain executives who listen well and to mimic their behavior.

With persistence and practice, such a process can lead to lasting results. I know one Wall Street executive who sought to improve his empathy—specifically his ability to read people's reactions and see their perspectives. Before beginning his quest, the executive's subordinates were terrified of working with him. People even went so far as to hide bad news from him. Naturally, he was shocked when finally confronted with these facts. He went home and told his family—but they only con-firmed what he had heard at work. When their opinions on any given subject did not mesh with his, they, too, were frightened of him.

Enlisting the help of a coach, the executive went to work to heighten his empathy through practice and feedback. His first step was to take a vacation to a foreign country where he did not speak the language. While there, he monitored his reactions to the unfamiliar and his openness to people who were different from him. When he returned home, humbled by his week abroad, the executive asked his coach to shadow him for parts of the day, several times a week, to critique how he treated people with new or different perspectives. At the same time, he consciously used on-the-job interactions as opportunities to practice "hearing" ideas that differed from his. Finally, the executive had himself videotaped in meetings and asked those who worked for and with him to critique his ability to acknowledge and understand the feelings of others. It took several months, but the executive's emotional intelligence did ultimately rise, and the improvement was reflected in his overall performance on the job.

It's important to emphasize that building one's emotional intelligence cannot—will not—happen without sincere desire and concerted effort. A brief seminar won't help; nor can one buy a how-to manual. It is much harder to learn to empathize—to internalize empathy as a natural response to people—than it is to become adept at regression analysis. But it can be done. "Nothing great was ever achieved without enthusiasm," wrote Ralph Waldo Emerson. If your goal is to become a real leader, these words can serve as a guidepost in your efforts to develop high emotional intelligence.

SELF-AWARENESS

Self-awareness is the first component of emotional intelligence—which makes sense when one considers that the Delphic oracle gave the advice to "know thyself" thousands of years ago. Self-awareness means having a deep understanding of one's emotions, strengths, weaknesses, needs, and drives. People with strong self-awareness are neither overly critical nor unrealistically hopeful. Rather, they are honest—with themselves and with others.

People who have a high degree of self-awareness recognize how their feelings affect them, other people, and their job performance. Thus, a self-aware person who knows that tight deadlines bring out the worst in him plans his time carefully and gets his work done well in advance. Another person with high self-awareness will be able to work with a demanding client. She will understand the client's impact on her moods and the deeper reasons for her frustration. "Their trivial demands take us away from the real work that needs to be done," she might explain. And she will go one step further and turn her anger into something constructive.

Self-awareness extends to a person's understanding of his or her values and goals. Someone who is highly self-aware knows where he is headed and why; so, for example, he will be able to be firm in turning down a job offer that is tempting financially but does not fit with his principles or long-term goals. A person who lacks self-awareness is apt to make decisions that bring on inner turmoil by treading on buried values. "The money looked good, so I signed on," someone might say two years into a job, "but the work means so little to me that I'm constantly bored." The decisions of self-aware people mesh with their values; consequently, they often find work to be energizing.

How can one recognize self-awareness? First and foremost, it shows itself as candor and an ability to assess oneself realistically. People with high self-awareness are able to speak accurately and openly—although not necessarily effusively or confessionally—about their emotions and the impact they have on their work. For instance, one manager I know of was skeptical about a new personal-shopper service that her company, a major department-store chain, was about to introduce. Without prompting from her team or her boss, she offered them an explanation: "It's hard for me to get behind the rollout of this service," she admitted, "because I really wanted to run the project, but I wasn't selected. Bear with me while I deal with that." The manager did indeed examine her feelings; a week later, she was supporting the project fully.

Such self-knowledge often shows itself in the hiring process. Ask a candidate to describe a time he got carried away by his feelings and did something he later regretted. Self-aware candidates will be frank in admitting to failure—and will often tell their tales with a smile. One of the hallmarks of self-awareness is a self-deprecating sense of humor.

Self-awareness can also be identified during performance reviews. Self-aware people know—and are comfortable talking about—their limitations and strengths, and they often demonstrate a thirst for constructive criticism. By contrast, people with low self-awareness interpret the message that they need to improve as a threat or a sign of failure.

Self-aware people can also be recognized by their self-confidence. They have a firm grasp of their capabilities and are less likely to set themselves up to fail by, for example, overstretching on assignments. They know, too, when to ask for help. And the risks they take on the job are calculated. They won't ask for a challenge that they know they can't handle alone. They'll play to their strengths.

Consider the actions of a midlevel employee who was invited to sit in on a strategy meeting with her company's top executives. Although she was the most junior person in the room, she did not sit there quietly, listening in awestruck or fearful silence. She knew she had a head for clear logic and the skill to present ideas persuasively, and she offered cogent suggestions about the company's strategy. At the same time, her self-awareness stopped her from wandering into territory where she knew she was weak.

Despite the value of having self-aware people in the workplace, my research indicates that senior executives don't often give self-awareness the credit it deserves when they look for potential leaders. Many executives mistake candor about feelings for "wimpiness" and fail to give due respect to employees who openly acknowledge their shortcomings. Such people are too readily dismissed as "not tough enough" to lead others.

In fact, the opposite is true. In the first place, people generally admire and respect candor. Furthermore, leaders are constantly required to make judgment calls that require a candid assessment of capabilities—their own and those of others. Do we have the management expertise to acquire a competitor? Can we launch a new product within six months? People who assess themselves honestly—that is, self-aware people—are well suited to do the same for the organizations they run.

SELF-REGULATION

Biological impulses drive our emotions. We cannot do away with them—but we can do much to manage them. Self-regulation, which is like an ongoing inner conversation, is the component of emotional intelligence that frees us from being prisoners of our feelings. People engaged in such a conversation feel bad moods and emotional impulses just as everyone else does, but they find ways to control them and even to channel them in useful ways.

Imagine an executive who has just watched a team of his employees present a botched analysis to the company's board of directors. In the gloom that follows, the executive might find himself tempted to pound on the table in anger or kick over a chair. He could leap up and scream at the group. Or he might maintain a grim silence, glaring at everyone before stalking off.

But if he had a gift for self-regulation, he would choose a different approach. He would pick his words carefully, acknowledging the team's poor performance without rushing to any hasty judgment. He would then step back to consider the reasons for the failure. Are they personal—a lack of effort? Are there any mitigating factors? What was his role in the debacle? After considering these questions, he would call the team together, lay out the incident's consequences, and offer his feelings about it. He would then present his analysis of the problem and a well-considered solution.

Why does self-regulation matter so much for leaders? First of all, people who are in control of their feelings and impulses— that is, people who are reasonable—are able to create an environment of trust and fairness. In such an environment, politics and infighting are sharply reduced and productivity is high. Talented people flock to the organization and aren't tempted to leave. And self-regulation has a trickle-down effect. No one wants to be known as a hot-head when the boss is known for her calm approach. Fewer bad moods at the top mean fewer throughout the organization.

Second, self-regulation is important for competitive reasons. Everyone knows that business today is rife with ambiguity and change. Companies merge and break apart regularly. Technology transforms work at a dizzying pace. People who have mastered their emotions are able to roll with the changes. When a new program is announced, they don't panic; instead, they are able to suspend judgment, seek out information, and listen to the executives as they explain the new program. As the initiative moves forward, these people are able to move with it.

Sometimes they even lead the way. Consider the case of a manager at a large manufacturing company. Like her colleagues, she had used a certain software program for five years. The program drove how she collected and reported data and how she thought about the company's strategy. One day, senior executives announced that a new program was to be installed that would radically change how information was gathered and assessed within the organization. While many people in the company complained bitterly about how disruptive the change would be, the manager mulled over the reasons for the new program and was convinced of its potential to improve performance. She eagerly attended training sessions—some of her colleagues refused to do so—and was eventually promoted to run several divisions, in part because she used the new technology so effectively.

I want to push the importance of self-regulation to leadership even further and make the case that it enhances integrity, which is not only a personal virtue but also an organizational strength. Many of the bad things that happen in companies are a function of impulsive behavior. People rarely plan to exaggerate profits, pad expense accounts, dip into the till, or abuse power for selfish ends. Instead, an opportunity presents itself, and people with low impulse control just say yes.

By contrast, consider the behavior of the senior executive at a large food company. The executive was scrupulously honest in his negotiations with local distributors. He would routinely lay out his cost structure in detail, thereby giving the distributors a realistic understanding of the company's pricing. This approach meant the executive couldn't always drive a hard bargain. Now, on occasion, he felt the urge to increase profits by withholding information about the company's costs. But he challenged that impulse—he saw that it made more sense in the long run to counteract it. His emotional self-regulation paid off in strong, lasting relationships with distributors that benefited the company more than any short-term financial gains would have.

The signs of emotional self-regulation, therefore, are easy to see: a propensity for reflection and thoughtfulness; comfort with ambiguity and change; and integrity—an ability to say no to impulsive urges.

Like self-awareness, self-regulation often does not get its due. People who can master their emotions are sometimes seen as cold fish—their considered responses are taken as a lack of passion. People with fiery temperaments are frequently thought of as "classic" leaders—their outbursts are considered hallmarks of charisma and power. But when such people make it to the top, their impulsiveness often works against them. In my research, extreme displays of negative emotion have never emerged as a driver of good leadership.

MOTIVATION

If there is one trait that virtually all effective leaders have, it is motivation. They are driven to achieve beyond expectations—their own and everyone else's. The key word here is *achieve*. Plenty of people are motivated by external factors, such as a big salary or the status that comes from having an impressive title or being part of a prestigious company.

By contrast, those with leadership potential are motivated by a deeply embedded desire to achieve for the sake of achievement.

If you are looking for leaders, how can you identify people who are motivated by the drive to achieve rather than by external rewards? The first sign is a passion for the work itself—such people seek out creative challenges, love to learn, and take great pride in a job well done. They also display an unflagging energy to do things better. People with such energy often seem restless with the status quo. They are persistent with their questions about why things are done one way rather than another; they are eager to explore new approaches to their work.

A cosmetics company manager, for example, was frustrated that he had to wait two weeks to get sales results from people in the field. He finally tracked down an automated phone system that would beep each of his salespeople at 5 p.m. every day. An automated message then prompted them to punch in their numbers—how many calls and sales they had made that day. The system shortened the feedback time on sales results from weeks to hours.

That story illustrates two other common traits of people who are driven to achieve. They are forever raising the performance bar, and they like to keep score. Take the performance bar first. During performance reviews, people with high levels of motivation might ask to be "stretched" by their superiors.

Of course, an employee who combines self-awareness with internal motivation will recognize her limits—but she won't settle for objectives that seem too easy to fulfill.

And it follows naturally that people who are driven to do better also want a way of tracking progress—their own, their team's, and their company's. Whereas people with low achievement motivation are often fuzzy about results, those with high achievement motivation often keep score by tracking such hard measures as profitability or market share. I know of a money manager who starts and ends his day on the Internet, gauging the performance of his stock fund against four industry-set benchmarks.

Interestingly, people with high motivation remain optimistic even when the score is against them. In such cases, self-regulation combines with achievement motivation to overcome the frustration and depression that come after a setback or failure. Take the case of an another portfolio manager at a large investment company. After several successful years, her fund tumbled for three consecutive quarters, leading three large institutional clients to shift their business elsewhere.

Some executives would have blamed the nosedive on circumstances outside their control; others might have seen the setback as evidence of personal failure. This portfolio manager, however, saw an opportunity to prove she could lead a turnaround. Two years later, when she was promoted to a very senior level in the company, she described the experience as "the best thing that ever happened to me; I learned so much from it."

Executives trying to recognize high levels of achievement motivation in their people can look for one last piece of evidence: commitment to the organization. When people love their jobs for the work itself, they often feel committed to the organizations that make that work possible. Committed employees are likely to stay with an organization even when they are pursued by headhunters waving money.

It's not difficult to understand how and why a motivation to achieve translates into strong leadership. If you set the performance bar high for yourself, you will do the same for the organization when you are in a position to do so. Likewise, a drive to surpass goals and an interest in keeping score can be contagious. Leaders with these traits can often build a team of managers around them with the same traits. And of course, optimism and organizational commitment are fundamental to leadership—just try to imagine running a company without them.

EMPATHY

Of all the dimensions of emotional intelligence, empathy is the most easily recognized. We have all felt the empathy of a sensitive teacher or friend; we have all been struck by its absence in an unfeeling coach or boss. But when it comes to business, we rarely hear people praised, let alone rewarded, for their empathy. The very word seems unbusinesslike, out of place amid the tough realities of the marketplace.

But empathy doesn't mean a kind of "I'm OK, you're OK" mushiness. For a leader, that is, it doesn't mean adopting other people's emotions as one's own and trying to please everybody. That would be a nightmare—it would make action impossible. Rather, empathy means thoughtfully considering employees' feelings—along with other factors—in the process of making intelligent decisions.

For an example of empathy in action, consider what happened when two giant brokerage companies merged, creating redundant jobs in all their divisions. One division manager called his people together and gave a gloomy speech that emphasized the number of people who would soon be fired. The manager of another division gave his people a different kind of speech. He was up-front about his own worry and confusion, and he promised to keep people informed and to treat everyone fairly.

The difference between these two managers was empathy. The first manager was too worried about his own fate to consider the feelings of his anxiety-stricken colleagues. The second knew intuitively what his people were feeling, and he acknowledged their fears with his words. Is it any surprise that the first manager saw his division sink as many demoralized people, especially the most talented, departed? By contrast, the second manager continued to be a strong leader, his best people stayed, and his division remained as productive as ever.

Empathy is particularly important today as a component of leadership for at least three reasons: the increasing use of teams; the rapid pace of globalization; and the growing need to retain talent.

Consider the challenge of leading a team. As anyone who has ever been a part of one can attest, teams are cauldrons of bubbling emotions. They are often charged with reaching a consensus—which is hard enough with two people and much more difficult as the numbers increase. Even in groups with as few as four or five members, alliances form and clashing agendas get set. A team's leader must be able to sense and understand the viewpoints of everyone around the table.

That's exactly what a marketing manager at a large information technology company was able to do when she was appointed to lead a troubled team. The group was in turmoil, overloaded by work and missing deadlines. Tensions were high among the members. Tinkering with procedures was not enough to bring the group together and make it an effective part of the company.

So the manager took several steps. In a series of one-on-one sessions, she took the time to listen to everyone in the group—what was frustrating them, how they rated their colleagues, whether they felt they had been ignored. And then she directed the team in a way that brought it together: She encouraged people to speak more openly about their frustrations, and she helped people raise constructive complaints during meetings. In short, her empathy allowed her to understand her team's emotional makeup. The result was not just heightened collaboration among members but also added business, as the team was called on for help by a wider range of internal clients.

Globalization is another reason for the rising importance of empathy for business leaders. Cross-cultural dialogue can easily lead to miscues and misunderstandings.

Empathy is an antidote. People who have it are attuned to subtleties in body language; they can hear the message beneath the words being spoken. Beyond that, they have a deep understanding of both the existence and the importance of cultural and ethnic differences.

Consider the case of an American consultant whose team had just pitched a project to a potential Japanese client. In its dealings with Americans, the team was accustomed to being bombarded with questions after such a proposal, but this time it was greeted with a long silence. Other members of the team, taking the silence as disapproval, were ready to pack and leave. The lead consultant gestured them to stop.

Although he was not particularly familiar with Japanese culture, he read the client's face and posture and sensed not rejection but interest—even deep consideration. He was right: When the client finally spoke, it was to give the consulting firm the job.

Finally, empathy plays a key role in the retention of talent, particularly in today's information economy. Leaders have always needed empathy to develop and keep good people, but today the stakes are higher. When good people leave, they take the company's knowledge with them.

That's where coaching and mentoring come in. It has repeatedly been shown that coaching and mentoring pay off not just in better performance but also in increased job satisfaction and decreased turnover. But what makes coaching and mentoring work best is the nature of the relationship. Outstanding coaches and mentors get inside the heads of the people they are helping. They sense how to give effective feedback. They know when to push for better performance and when to hold back. In the way they motivate their protégés, they demonstrate empathy in action.

In what is probably sounding like a refrain, let me repeat that empathy doesn't get much respect in business. People wonder how leaders can make hard decisions if they are "feeling" for all the people who will be affected. But leaders with empathy do more than sympathize with people around them: They use their knowledge to improve their companies in subtle but important ways.

SOCIAL SKILL

The first three components of emotional intelligence are self-management skills. The last two, empathy and social skill, concern a person's ability to manage relationships with others. As a component of emotional intelligence, social skill is not as simple as it sounds. It's not just a matter of friendliness, although people with high levels of social skill are rarely mean-spirited. Social skill, rather, is friendliness with a purpose: moving people in the direction you desire, whether that's agreement on a new marketing strategy or enthusiasm about a new product.

Socially skilled people tend to have a wide circle of acquaintances, and they have a knack for finding common ground with people of all kinds—a knack for building rapport. That doesn't mean they socialize continually; it means they work according to the assumption that nothing important gets done alone. Such people have a network in place when the time for action comes.

Social skill is the culmination of the other dimensions of emotional intelligence. People tend to be very effective at managing relationships when they can understand and control their own emotions and can empathize with the feelings of others. Even motivation contributes to social skill. Remember that people who are driven to achieve tend to be optimistic, even in the face of setbacks or failure. When people are upbeat, their "glow" is cast upon conversations and other social encounters. They are popular, and for good reason.

Because it is the outcome of the other dimensions of emotional intelligence, social skill is recognizable on the job in many ways that will by now sound familiar. Socially skilled people, for instance, are adept at managing teams—that's their empathy at work. Likewise, they are expert persuaders—a manifestation of self-awareness, self-regulation, and empathy combined. Given those skills, good persuaders know when to make an emotional plea, for instance, and when an appeal to reason will work better. And motivation, when publicly visible, makes such people excellent collaborators; their passion for the work spreads to others, and they are driven to find solutions.

But sometimes social skill shows itself in ways the other emotional intelligence components do not. For instance, socially skilled people may at times appear not to be working while at work. They seem to be idly schmoozing—chatting in the hallways with colleagues or joking around with people who are not even connected to their "real" jobs. Socially skilled people, however, don't think it makes sense to arbitrarily limit the scope of their relationships. They build bonds widely because they know that in these fluid times, they may need help someday from people they are just getting to know today.

For example, consider the case of an executive in the strategy department of a global computer manufacturer. By 1993, he was convinced that the company's future lay with the Internet. Over the course of the next year, he found kindred spirits and used his social skill to stitch together a virtual community that cut across levels, divisions, and nations. He then used this de facto team to put up a corporate Web site, among the first by a major company. And, on his own initiative, with no budget or formal status, he signed up the company to participate in an annual Internet industry convention. Calling on his allies and persuading various divisions to donate funds, he recruited more than 50 people from a dozen different units to represent the company at the convention.

Management took notice: Within a year of the conference, the executive's team formed the basis for the company's first Internet division, and he was formally put in charge of it. To get there, the executive had ignored conventional boundaries, forging and maintaining connections with people in every corner of the organization.

Is social skill considered a key leadership capability in most companies? The answer is yes, especially when compared with the other components of emotional intelligence. People seem to know intuitively that leaders need to manage relationships effectively; no leader is an island. After all, the leader's task is to get work done through other people, and social skill makes that possible. A leader who cannot express her empathy may as well not have it at all. And a leader's motivation will be useless if he cannot communicate his passion to the organization. Social skill allows leaders to put their emotional intelligence to work.

It would be foolish to assert that good old-fashioned IQ and technical ability are not important ingredients in strong leadership. But the recipe would not be complete without emotional intelligence. It was once thought that the components of emotional intelligence were "nice to have" in business leaders. But now we know that, for the sake of performance, these are ingredients that leaders "need to have."

It is fortunate, then, that emotional intelligence can be learned. The process is not easy. It takes time and, most of all, commitment. But the benefits that come from having a well-developed emotional intelligence, both for the individual and for the organization, make it worth the effort.

The five components of emotional intelligence at work

	Definition	Hallmarks
Self-awareness	The ability to recognize and understand your moods, emotions, and drives, as well as their effect on others	Self-confidence Realistic self-assessment Self-deprecating sense of humor
Self-regulation	The ability to control or redirect disruptive impulses and moods The propensity to suspend judgment—to think before acting	Trustworthiness and integrity Comfort with ambiguity Openness to change
Motivation	A passion to work for reasons that go beyond money or status A propensity to pursue goals with energy and persistence	Strong drive to achieve Optimism, even in the face of failure Organizational commitment

(continued)

	Definition	Hallmarks
Empathy	The ability to understand the emotional makeup of other people Skill in treating people according to their emotional reactions	Expertise in building and retaining talent Cross-cultural sensitivity Service to clients and customers
Social skill	Proficiency in managing relationships and building networks An ability to find common ground and build rapport	Effectiveness in leading change Persuasiveness Expertise in building and leading teams

Article Summary

Idea in Brief

What distinguishes great leaders from merely good ones? It isn't IQ or technical skills, says Daniel Goleman. It's **emotional intelligence**: a group of five skills that enable the best leaders to maximize their own *and* their followers' performance. When senior managers at one company had a critical mass of EI capabilities, their divisions outperformed yearly earnings goals by 20%.

The EI skills are:

- *Self-awareness*—knowing one's strengths, weaknesses, drives, values, and impact on others

- *Self-regulation*—controlling or redirecting disruptive impulses and moods

- *Motivation*—relishing achievement for its own sake

- *Empathy*—understanding other people's emotional makeup

- *Social skill*—building rapport with others to move them in desired directions

We're each born with certain levels of EI skills. But we can strengthen these abilities through persistence, practice, and feedback from colleagues or coaches.

The Focused
Leader

A primary task of leadership is to direct attention. To do so, leaders must learn to focus their own attention. When we speak about being focused, we commonly mean thinking about one thing while filtering out distractions. But a wealth of recent research in neuroscience shows that we focus in many ways, for different purposes, drawing on different neural pathways—some of which work in concert, while others tend to stand in opposition.

Grouping these modes of attention into three broad buckets—focusing on *yourself*, focusing on *others*, and focusing on *the wider world*—sheds new light on the practice of many essential leadership skills. Focusing inward and focusing constructively on others helps leaders cultivate the primary elements of emotional intelligence. A fuller understanding of how they focus on the wider world can improve their ability to devise strategy, innovate, and manage organizations.

Every leader needs to cultivate this triad of awareness, in abundance and in the proper balance, because a failure to focus inward leaves you rudderless, a failure to focus on others renders you clueless, and a failure to focus outward may leave you blindsided.

FOCUSING ON YOURSELF

Emotional intelligence begins with self-awareness—getting in touch with your inner voice. Leaders who heed their inner voices can draw on more resources to make better decisions and connect with their authentic selves. But what does that entail? A look at how people focus inward can make this abstract concept more concrete.

Self-awareness

Hearing your inner voice is a matter of paying careful attention to internal physiological signals. These subtle cues are monitored by the insula, which is tucked behind the frontal lobes of the brain.

Attention given to any part of the body amps up the insula's sensitivity to that part. Tune in to your heartbeat, and the insula activates more neurons in that circuitry. How well people can sense their heartbeats has, in fact, become a standard way to measure their self-awareness.

Gut feelings are messages from the insula and the amygdala, which the neuroscientist Antonio Damasio, of the University of Southern California, calls *somatic markers*. Those messages are sensations that something "feels" right or wrong. Somatic markers simplify decision making by guiding our attention toward better options. They're hardly foolproof (how often was that feeling that you left the stove on correct?), so the more comprehensively we read them, the better we use our intuition. (See "Are You Skimming This Sidebar?")

Consider, for example, the implications of an analysis of interviews conducted by a group of British researchers with 118 professional traders and 10 senior managers at four City of London investment banks. The most successful traders (whose annual income averaged £500,000) were neither the ones who relied entirely on analytics nor the ones who just went with their guts. They focused on a full range of emotions, which they used to judge the value of their intuition. When they suffered losses, they acknowledged their anxiety, became more cautious, and took fewer risks. The least successful traders (whose income averaged only £100,000) tended to ignore their anxiety and keep going with their guts. Because they failed to heed a wider array of internal signals, they were misled.

Zeroing in on sensory impressions of ourselves in the moment is one major element of self-awareness. But another is critical to leadership: combining our experiences across time into a coherent view of our authentic selves.

To be authentic is to be the same person to others as you are to yourself. In part that entails paying attention to what others think of you, particularly people whose opinions you esteem and who will be candid in their feedback. A variety of focus that is useful here is *open awareness*, in which we broadly notice what's going on around us without getting caught up in or swept away by any particular thing. In this mode we don't judge, censor, or tune out; we simply perceive.

Leaders who are more accustomed to giving input than to receiving it may find this tricky. Someone who has trouble sustaining open awareness typically gets snagged by irritating details, such as fellow travelers in the airport security line who take forever getting their carry-ons into the scanner. Someone who can keep her attention in open mode will notice the travelers but not worry about them, and will take in more of her surroundings. (See the sidebar "Expand Your Awareness.")

Of course, being open to input doesn't guarantee that someone will provide it. Sadly, life affords us few chances to learn how others really see us, and even fewer for executives as they rise through the ranks. That may be why one of the most popular and overenrolled courses at Harvard Business School is Bill George's Authentic Leadership Development, in which George has created what he calls True North groups to heighten this aspect of self-awareness.

These groups (which anyone can form) are based on the precept that self-knowledge begins with self-revelation. Accordingly, they are open and intimate, "a safe place," George explains, "where members can discuss personal issues they do not feel they can raise elsewhere—often not even with their closest family members." What good does that do? "We don't know who we are until we hear ourselves speaking the story of our lives to those we trust," George says. It's a structured way to match our view of our true selves with the views our most trusted colleagues have— an external check on our authenticity.

Self-control

"Cognitive control" is the scientific term for putting one's attention where one wants it and keeping it there in the face of temptation to wander. This focus is one aspect of the brain's executive function, which is located in the prefrontal cortex. A colloquial term for it is "willpower."

Cognitive control enables executives to pursue a goal despite distractions and setbacks. The same neural circuitry that allows such a single-minded pursuit of goals also manages unruly emotions. Good cognitive control can be seen in people who stay calm in a crisis, tame their own agitation, and recover from a debacle or defeat.

Decades' worth of research demonstrates the singular importance of willpower to leadership success. Particularly compelling is a longitudinal study tracking the fates of all 1,037 children born during a single year in the 1970s in the New Zealand city of Dunedin. For several years during childhood the children were given a battery of tests of willpower, including the psychologist Walter

Mischel's legendary "marshmallow test"—a choice between eating one marshmallow right away and getting two by waiting 15 minutes. In Mischel's experiments, roughly a third of children grab the marshmallow on the spot, another third hold out for a while longer, and a third manage to make it through the entire quarter hour.

Years later, when the children in the Dunedin study were in their 30s and all but 4% of them had been tracked down again, the researchers found that those who'd had the cognitive control to resist the marshmallow longest were significantly healthier, more successful financially, and more law-abiding than the ones who'd been unable to hold out at all. In fact, statistical analysis showed that a child's level of self-control was a more powerful predictor of financial success than IQ, social class, or family circumstance.

How we focus holds the key to exercising willpower, Mischel says. Three subvarieties of cognitive control are at play when you pit self-restraint against self-gratification: the ability to voluntarily disengage your focus from an object of desire; the ability to resist distraction so that you don't gravitate back to that object; and the ability to concentrate on the future goal and imagine how good you will feel when you achieve it. As adults the children of Dunedin may have been held hostage to their younger selves, but they need not have been, because the power to focus can be developed. (See the sidebar "Learning Self-Restraint.")

FOCUSING ON OTHERS

The word "attention" comes from the Latin *attendere*, meaning "to reach toward." This is a perfect definition of focus on others, which is the foundation of empathy and of an ability to build social relationships— the second and third pillars of emotional intelligence.

Executives who can effectively focus on others are easy to recognize. They are the ones who find common ground, whose opinions carry the most weight, and with whom other people want to work. They emerge as natural leaders regardless of organizational or social rank.

The empathy triad

We talk about empathy most commonly as a single attribute. But a close look at where leaders are focusing when they exhibit it reveals three distinct kinds, each important for leadership effectiveness:

- *Cognitive empathy*: the ability to understand another person's perspective;

- *Emotional empathy*: the ability to feel what someone else feels;

- *Empathic concern*: the ability to sense what another person needs from you.

Cognitive empathy enables leaders to explain themselves in meaningful ways—a skill essential to getting the best performance from their direct reports. Contrary to what you might expect, exercising cognitive empathy requires leaders to think about feelings rather than to feel them directly.

An inquisitive nature feeds cognitive empathy. As one successful executive with this trait puts it, "I've always just wanted to learn everything, to understand anybody that I was around—why they thought what they did, why they did what they did, what worked for them, and what didn't work." But cognitive empathy is also an outgrowth of self-awareness. The executive circuits that allow us to think about our own thoughts and to monitor the feelings that flow from them let us apply the same reasoning to other people's minds when we choose to direct our attention that way.

Emotional empathy is important for effective mentoring, managing clients, and reading group dynamics. It springs from ancient parts of the brain beneath the cortex—the amygdala, the hypothalamus, the hippocampus, and the orbitofrontal cortex—that allow us to feel fast without thinking deeply. They tune us in by arousing in our bodies the emotional states of others: I literally feel your pain. My brain patterns match up with yours when I listen to you tell a gripping story. As Tania Singer, the director of the social neuroscience department at the Max

Planck Institute for Human Cognitive and Brain Sciences, in Leipzig, says, "You need to understand your own feelings to understand the feelings of others." Accessing your capacity for emotional empathy depends on combining two kinds of attention: a deliberate focus on your own echoes of someone else's feelings and an open awareness of that person's face, voice, and other external signs of emotion. (See the sidebar "When Empathy Needs to Be Learned.")

Empathic concern, which is closely related to emotional empathy, enables you to sense not just how people feel but what they need from you. It's what you want in your doctor, your spouse—and your boss. Empathic concern has its roots in the circuitry that compels parents' attention to their children. Watch where people's eyes go when someone brings an adorable baby into a room, and you'll see this mammalian brain center leaping into action.

One neural theory holds that the response is triggered in the amygdala by the brain's radar for sensing danger and in the prefrontal cortex by the release of oxytocin, the chemical for caring. This implies that empathic concern is a double-edged feeling. We intuitively experience the distress of another as our own. But in deciding whether we will meet that person's needs, we deliberately weigh how much we value his or her well-being.

Getting this intuition-deliberation mix right has great implications. Those whose sympathetic feelings become too strong may themselves suffer. In the helping professions, this can lead to compassion fatigue; in executives, it can create distracting feelings of anxiety about people and circumstances that are beyond anyone's control. But those who protect themselves by deadening their feelings may lose touch with empathy. Empathic concern requires us to manage our personal distress without numbing ourselves to the pain of others. (See the sidebar "When Empathy Needs to Be Controlled.")

What's more, some lab research suggests that the appropriate application of empathic concern is critical to making moral judgments. Brain scans have revealed that when volunteers listened to tales of people subjected to physical pain, their own brain centers for experiencing such pain lit up instantly. But if the story was about psychological suffering, the higher brain centers involved in empathic concern and compassion took longer to activate. Some time is needed to grasp the psychological and moral dimensions of a situation. The more distracted we are, the less we can cultivate the subtler forms of empathy and compassion.

Building relationships

People who lack social sensitivity are easy to spot—at least for other people. They are the clueless among us. The CFO who is technically competent but bullies some people, freezes out others, and plays favorites—but when you point out what he has just done, shifts the blame, gets angry, or thinks that you're the problem—is not trying to be a jerk; he's utterly unaware of his shortcomings.

Social sensitivity appears to be related to cognitive empathy. Cognitively empathic executives do better at overseas assignments, for instance, presumably because they quickly pick up implicit norms and learn the unique mental models of a new culture. Attention to social context lets us act with skill no matter what the situation, instinctively follow the universal algorithm for etiquette, and behave in ways that put others at ease. (In another age this might have been called good manners.)

Circuitry that converges on the anterior hippocampus reads social context and leads us intuitively to act differently with, say, our college buddies than with our families or our colleagues. In concert with the deliberative prefrontal cortex, it squelches the impulse to do something inappropriate. Accordingly, one brain test for sensitivity to context assesses the function of the hippocampus. The University of Wisconsin neuroscientist Richard Davidson hypothesizes that people who are most alert to social situations exhibit stronger activity and more connections between the hippocampus and the prefrontal cortex than those who just can't seem to get it right.

The same circuits may be at play when we map social networks in a group—a skill that lets us navigate the relationships in those networks well. People who excel at organizational influence can not only sense the flow of personal connections but also name the people whose opinions hold most sway, and so focus on persuading those who will persuade others.

Alarmingly, research suggests that as people rise through the ranks and gain power, their ability to perceive and maintain personal connections tends to suffer a sort of psychic attrition. In studying encounters between people of varying status, Dacher Keltner, a psychologist at Berkeley, has found that higher-ranking individuals consistently focus their gaze less on lower-ranking people and are more likely to interrupt or to monopolize the conversation.

In fact, mapping attention to power in an organization gives a clear indication of hierarchy: The longer it takes Person A to respond to Person B, the more relative power Person A has. Map response times across an entire organization, and you'll get a remarkably accurate chart of social standing. The boss leaves e-mails unanswered for hours; those lower down respond within minutes. This is so predictable that an algorithm for it—called automated social hierarchy detection—has been developed at Columbia University. Intelligence agencies reportedly are applying the algorithm to suspected terrorist gangs to piece together chains of influence and identify central figures.

But the real point is this: Where we see ourselves on the social ladder sets the default for how much attention we pay. This should be a warning to top executives, who need to respond to fast-moving competitive situations by tapping the full range of ideas and talents within an organization. Without a deliberate shift in attention, their natural inclination may be to ignore smart ideas from the lower ranks.

FOCUSING ON THE WIDER WORLD

Leaders with a strong outward focus are not only good listeners but also good questioners. They are visionaries who can sense the far-flung consequences of local decisions and imagine how the choices they make today will play out in the future. They are open to the surprising ways in which seemingly unrelated data can inform their central interests. Melinda Gates offered up a cogent example when she remarked on *60 Minutes* that her husband was the kind of person who would read an entire book about fertilizer. Charlie Rose asked, Why fertilizer? The connection was obvious to Bill Gates, who is constantly looking for technological advances that can save lives on a massive scale. "A few billion people would have to die if we hadn't come up with fertilizer," he replied.

Focusing on strategy

Any business school course on strategy will give you the two main elements: exploitation of your current advantage and exploration for new ones. Brain scans that were performed on 63 seasoned business decision makers as they pursued or switched between exploitative and exploratory strategies revealed the specific circuits involved. Not surprisingly, exploitation requires concentration on the job at hand, whereas exploration demands open awareness to recognize new possibilities. But exploitation is accompanied by activity in the brain's circuitry for anticipation and reward. In other words, it feels good to coast along in a familiar routine. When we switch to exploration, we have to make a deliberate cognitive effort to disengage from that routine in order to roam widely and pursue fresh paths.

What keeps us from making that effort? Sleep deprivation, drinking, stress, and mental over-load all interfere with the executive circuitry used to make the cognitive switch. To sustain the outward focus that leads to innovation, we need some uninterrupted time in which to reflect and refresh our focus.

The wellsprings of innovation

In an era when almost everyone has access to the same information, new value arises from putting ideas together in novel ways and asking smart questions that open up untapped potential. Moments before we have a creative insight, the brain shows a third-of-a-second spike in gamma waves, indicating the synchrony of far-flung brain cells. The more neurons firing in sync, the bigger the spike. Its timing suggests that what's happening is the formation of a new neural network—presumably creating a fresh association.

But it would be making too much of this to see gamma waves as a secret to creativity. A classic model of creativity suggests how the various modes of attention play key roles. First we prepare our minds by gathering a wide variety of pertinent information, and then we alternate between concentrating intently on the problem and letting our minds wander freely. Those activities translate roughly into vigilance, when while immersing ourselves in all kinds of input, we remain alert for anything relevant to the problem at hand; selective attention to the specific creative challenge; and open awareness, in which we allow our minds to associate freely and the solution to emerge spontaneously. (That's why so many fresh ideas come to people in the shower or out for a walk or a run.)

The dubious gift of systems awareness

If people are given a quick view of a photo of lots of dots and asked to guess how many there are, the strong systems thinkers in the group tend to make the best estimates. This skill shows up in those who are good at designing software, assembly lines, matrix organizations, or interventions to save failing ecosystems—it's a very powerful gift indeed. After all, we live within extremely complex systems. But, suggests the Cambridge University psychologist Simon Baron-Cohen (a cousin of Sacha's), in a small but significant number of people, a strong systems awareness is coupled with an empathy deficit—a blind spot for what other people are thinking and feeling and for reading social situations. For that reason, although people with a superior systems understanding are organizational assets, they are not necessarily effective leaders.

An executive at one bank explained to me that it has created a separate career ladder for systems analysts so that they can progress in status and salary on the basis of their systems smarts alone. That way, the bank can consult them as needed while recruiting leaders from a different pool— one containing people with emotional intelligence.

PUTTING IT ALL TOGETHER

For those who don't want to end up similarly compartmentalized, the message is clear. A focused leader is not the person concentrating on the three most important priorities of the year, or the most brilliant systems thinker, or the one most in tune with the corporate culture. Focused leaders can command the full range of their own attention: They are in touch with their inner feelings, they can control their impulses, they are aware of how others see them, they understand what others need from them, they can weed out distractions and also allow their minds to roam widely, free of preconceptions.

This is challenging. But if great leadership were a paint-by-numbers exercise, great leaders would be more common. Practically every form of focus can be strengthened. What it takes is not talent so much as diligence—a willingness to exercise the attention circuits of the brain just as we exercise our analytic skills and other systems of the body.

The link between attention and excellence remains hidden most of the time. Yet attention is the basis of the most essential of leadership skills—emotional, organizational, and strategic intelligence. And never has it been under greater assault. The constant onslaught of incoming data leads to sloppy shortcuts—triaging our e-mail by reading only the subject lines, skipping many of our voice mails, skimming memos and reports. Not only do our habits of attention make us less effective, but the sheer volume of all those messages leaves us too little time to reflect on what they really mean. This was foreseen more than 40 years ago by the Nobel Prize–winning economist Herbert Simon. Information "consumes the attention of its recipients," he wrote in 1971. "Hence a wealth of information creates a poverty of attention."

My goal here is to place attention center stage so that you can direct it where you need it when you need it. Learn to master your attention, and you will be in command of where you, and your organization, focus.

Are You Skimming This Sidebar?

Do you have trouble remembering what someone has just told you in conversation? Did you drive to work this morning on autopilot? Do you focus more on your smartphone than on the person you're having lunch with?

Attention is a mental muscle; like any other muscle, it can be strengthened through the right kind of exercise. The fundamental rep for building deliberate attention is simple: When your mind wanders, notice that it has wandered, bring it back to your desired point of focus, and keep it there as long as you can. That basic exercise is at the root of virtually every kind of meditation. Meditation builds concentration and calmness and facilitates recovery from the agitation of stress.

So does a video game called Tenacity, developed by a design group and neuroscientists at the University of Wisconsin. The game offers a leisurely journey through any of half a dozen scenes, from a barren desert to a fantasy staircase spiraling heavenward. At the beginner's level you tap an iPad screen with one finger every time you exhale; the challenge is to tap two fingers with every fifth breath. As you move to higher levels, you're presented with more distractions—a helicopter flies into view, a plane does a flip, a flock of birds suddenly scuds by.

When players are attuned to the rhythm of their breathing, they experience the strengthening of selective attention as a feeling of calm focus, as in meditation. Stanford University is exploring that connection at its Calming Technology Lab, which is developing relaxing devices, such as a belt that detects your breathing rate. Should a chock-full in-box, for instance, trigger what has been called e-mail apnea, an iPhone app can guide you through exercises to calm your breathing and your mind.

Expand Your Awareness

Just as a camera lens can be set narrowly on a single point or more widely to take in a panoramic view, you can focus tightly or expansively.

One measure of open awareness presents people with a stream of letters and numbers, such as S, K, O, E, 4, R, T, 2, H, P. In scanning the stream, many people will notice the first number, 4, but after that their attention blinks. Those firmly in open awareness mode will register the second number as well.

Strengthening the ability to maintain open awareness requires leaders to do something that verges on the unnatural: Cultivate at least sometimes a willingness to not be in control, not offer up their own views, not judge others. That's less a matter of deliberate action than of attitude adjustment.

One path to making that adjustment is through the classic power of positive thinking, because pessimism narrows our focus, whereas positive emotions widen our attention and our receptiveness to the new and unexpected. A simple way to shift into positive mode is to ask yourself, "If everything worked out perfectly in my life, what would I be doing in 10 years?" Why is that effective? Because when you're in an upbeat mood, the University of Wisconsin neuroscientist Richard Davidson has found, your brain's left prefrontal area lights up. That area harbors the circuitry that reminds us how great we'll feel when we reach some long-sought goal.

"Talking about positive goals and dreams activates brain centers that open you up to new possibilities," says Richard Boyatzis, a psychologist at Case Western Reserve. "But if you change the conversation to what you should do to fix yourself, it closes you down . . . You need the negative to survive, but the positive to thrive."

Learning Self-Restraint

Quick, now. Here's a test of cognitive control. In what direction is the middle arrow in each row pointing?

→ → → ← ←
→ ← ← ← ←
→ → ← → →

The test, called the Eriksen Flanker Task, gauges your susceptibility to distraction. When it's taken under laboratory conditions, differences of a thousandth of a second can be detected in the speed with which subjects perceive which direction the middle arrows are pointing. The stronger their cognitive control, the less susceptible they are to distraction.

Interventions to strengthen cognitive control can be as unsophisticated as a game of

Simon Says or Red Light—any exercise in which you are asked to stop on cue. Research suggests that the better a child gets at playing Musical Chairs, the stronger his or her prefrontal wiring for cognitive control will become.

Operating on a similarly simple principle is a social and emotional learning (SEL) method that's used to strengthen cognitive control in schoolchildren across the United States. When confronted by an upsetting problem, the children are told to think of a traffic signal. The red light means stop, calm down, and think before you act. The yellow light means slow down and think of several possible solutions. The green light means try out a plan and see how it works. Thinking in these terms allows the children to shift away from amygdala-driven impulses to prefrontal-driven deliberate behavior.

It's never too late for adults to strengthen these circuits as well. Daily sessions of mindfulness practice work in a way similar to Musical Chairs and SEL. In these sessions you focus your attention on your breathing and practice tracking your thoughts and feelings without getting swept away by them. Whenever you notice that your mind has wandered, you simply return it to your breath. It sounds easy—but try it for 10 minutes, and you'll find there's a learning curve.

When Empathy Needs to Be Learned

Emotional empathy can be developed. That's the conclusion suggested by research conducted with physicians by Helen Riess, the director of the Empathy and Relational Science Program at Boston's Massachusetts General Hospital. To help the physicians monitor themselves, she set up a program in which they learned to focus using deep, diaphragmatic breathing and to cultivate a certain detachment—to watch an interaction from the ceiling, as it were, rather than being lost in their own thoughts and feelings. "Suspending your own involvement to observe what's going on gives you a mindful awareness of the interaction without being completely reactive," says Riess. "You can see if your own physiology is charged up or balanced. You can notice what's transpiring in the situation." If a doctor realizes that she's feeling irritated, for instance, that may be a signal that the patient is bothered too.

Those who are utterly at a loss may be able to prime emotional empathy essentially by faking it until they make it, Riess adds. If you act in a caring way—looking people in the eye and paying attention to their expressions, even when you don't particularly want to—you may start to feel more engaged.

When Empathy Needs to Be Controlled

Getting a grip on our impulse to empathize with other people's feelings can help us make better decisions when someone's emotional flood threatens to overwhelm us.

Ordinarily, when we see someone pricked with a pin, our brains emit a signal indicating that our own pain centers are echoing that distress. But physicians learn in medical school to block even such automatic responses. Their attentional anesthetic seems to be deployed by the temporal-parietal junction and regions of the prefrontal cortex, a circuit that boosts concentration by tuning out emotions. That's what is happening in your brain when you distance yourself from others in order to stay calm and help them. The same neural network kicks in when we see a problem in an emotionally overheated environment and need to focus on looking for a solution. If you're talking with someone who is upset, this system helps you understand the person's perspective intellectually by shifting from the heart-to-heart of emotional empathy to the head-to-heart of cognitive empathy.

Article Summary

Idea in Brief

The Problem
A primary task of leadership is to direct attention. To do so, leaders must learn to focus their own attention.

The Argument
People commonly think of "being focused" as filtering out distractions while concentrating on one thing. But a wealth of recent neuroscience

research shows that we focus attention in many ways, for different purposes, while drawing on different neural pathways.

The Solution

Every leader needs to cultivate a triad of awareness—an inward focus, a focus on others, and an outward focus. Focusing inward and focusing on others helps leaders cultivate emotional intelligence. Focusing outward can improve their ability to devise strategy, innovate, and manage organizations.

Leadership
That Gets
Results

Ask any group of businesspeople the question "What do effective leaders do?" and you'll hear a sweep of answers. Leaders set strategy; they motivate; they create a mission; they build a culture. Then ask "What should leaders do?" If the group is seasoned, you'll likely hear one response: The leader's singular job is to get results.

But how? The mystery of what leaders can and ought to do in order to spark the best performance from their people is age-old. In recent years, that mystery has spawned an entire cottage industry: Literally thousands of "leadership experts" have made careers of testing and coaching executives, all in pursuit of creating businesspeople who can turn bold objectives—be they strategic, financial, organizational, or all three—into reality.

Still, effective leadership eludes many people and organizations. One reason is that until recently, virtually no quantitative research has demonstrated which precise leadership behaviors yield positive results. Leadership experts proffer advice based on inference, experience, and instinct. Sometimes that advice is which precise leadership behaviors yield positive results. Sometimes that advice is right on target; sometimes it's not.

But new research by the consulting firm Hay/McBer, which draws on a random sample of 3,871 executives selected from a database of more than 20,000 executives worldwide, takes much of the mystery out of effective leadership. The research found six distinct leadership styles, each springing from different components of emotional intelligence. The styles, taken individually, appear to have a direct and unique impact on the working atmosphere of a company, division, or team, and in turn, on its financial performance. And perhaps most important, the research indicates that leaders with the best results do not rely on only one leadership style; they use most of them in a given week—seamlessly and in different measure—depending on the business situation. Imagine the styles, then, as the array of clubs in a golf pro's bag. Over the course of a game, the pro picks and chooses clubs based on the demands of the shot. Sometimes he has to ponder his selection, but usually it is automatic. The pro senses the challenge ahead, swiftly pulls out the right tool, and elegantly puts it to work. That's how high-impact leaders operate, too.

What are the six styles of leadership? None will shock workplace veterans. Indeed, each style, by name and brief description alone, will likely resonate with anyone who leads, is led, or as is the case with most of us, does both. *Coercive leaders* demand immediate compliance. *Authoritative leaders* mobilize people toward a vision. *Affiliative leaders* create emotional bonds and harmony. *Democratic leaders* build consensus through participation. *Pacesetting leaders* expect excellence and self-direction. And *coaching leaders* develop people for the future.

Close your eyes and you can surely imagine a colleague who uses any one of these styles. You most likely use at least one yourself. What is new in this research, then, is its implications for action. First, it offers a fine-grained understanding of how different leadership styles affect performance and results. Second, it offers clear guidance on when a manager should switch between them. It also strongly suggests that switching flexibly is well advised. New, too, is the research's finding that each leadership style springs from different components of emotional intelligence.

MEASURING LEADERSHIP'S IMPACT

It has been more than a decade since research first linked aspects of emotional intelligence to business results. The late David McClelland, a noted Harvard University psychologist, found that leaders with strengths in a critical mass of six or more emotional intelligence competencies were far more effective than peers who lacked such strengths. For instance, when he analyzed the performance of division heads at a global food and beverage company, he found that among leaders with this critical mass of competence, 87% placed in the top third for annual salary bonuses based on their business performance. More telling, their divisions on average outperformed yearly revenue targets by 15% to 20%. Those executives who lacked emotional intelligence were rarely rated as outstanding in their annual performance reviews, and their divisions underperformed by an average of almost 20%.

Our research set out to gain a more molecular view of the links among leadership and emotional intelligence, and climate and performance. A team of McClelland's colleagues headed by Mary Fontaine and Ruth Jacobs from Hay/McBer studied data about or observed thousands of executives, noting specific behaviors and their impact on climate. How did each individual motivate direct reports? Manage change initiatives? Handle crises? It was in a later phase of the research that we identified which emotional intelligence capabilities drive the six leadership styles. How does he rate in terms of self-control and social skill? Does a leader show high or low levels of empathy?

The team tested each executive's immediate sphere of influence for its climate. "Climate" is not an amorphous term. First defined by psychologists George Litwin and Richard Stringer and later refined by McClelland and his colleagues, it refers to six key factors that influence an organization's working environment: its flexibility—that is, how free employees feel to innovate unencumbered by red tape; their sense of responsibility to the organization; the level of standards that people set; the sense of accuracy about performance feedback and aptness of rewards; the clarity people have about mission and values; and finally, the level of commitment to a common purpose.

We found that all six leadership styles have a measurable effect on each aspect of climate. (For details, see the table "Getting Molecular: The Impact of Leadership Styles on Drivers of Climate.") Further, when we looked at the impact of climate on financial results—such as return on sales, revenue growth, efficiency, and profitability—we found a direct correlation between the two. Leaders who used styles that positively affected the climate had decidedly better financial results than those who did not. That is not to say that organizational climate is the only driver of performance. Economic conditions and competitive dynamics matter enormously. But our analysis strongly suggests that climate accounts for nearly a third of results. And that's simply too much of an impact to ignore.

THE STYLES IN DETAIL

Executives use six leadership styles, but only four of the six consistently have a positive effect on climate and results. Let's look then at each style of leadership in detail. (For a summary of the material that follows, see the table "The Six Leadership Styles at a Glance.")

The coercive style

The computer company was in crisis mode—its sales and profits were falling, its stock was losing value precipitously, and its shareholders were in an uproar. The board brought in a new CEO with a reputation as a turnaround artist. He set to work chopping jobs, selling off divisions, and making the tough decisions that should have been executed years before. The company was saved, at least in the short term.

From the start, though, the CEO created a reign of terror, bullying and demeaning his executives, roaring his displeasure at the slightest misstep. The company's top echelons were decimated not just by his erratic firings but also by defections. The CEO's direct reports, frightened by his tendency to blame the bearer of bad news, stopped bringing him any news at all. Morale was at an all-time low—a fact reflected in another downturn in the business after the short-term recovery. The CEO was eventually fired by the board of directors.

It's easy to understand why of all the leadership styles, the coercive one is the least effective in most situations. Consider what the style does to an organization's climate. Flexibility is the hardest hit. The leader's extreme top-down decision making kills new ideas on the vine. People feel so disrespected that they think, "I won't even bring my ideas up—they'll only be shot down." Likewise, people's sense of responsibility evaporates: Unable to act on their own initiative, they lose their sense of ownership and feel little accountability for their performance. Some become so resentful they adopt the attitude, "I'm not going to help this bastard."

Coercive leadership also has a damaging effect on the rewards system. Most high-performing workers are motivated by more than money—they seek the satisfaction of work well done. The coercive style erodes such pride. And finally, the style undermines one of the leader's prime tools—motivating people by showing them how their job fits into a grand, shared mission. Such a loss, measured in terms of diminished clarity and commitment, leaves people alienated from their own jobs, wondering, "How does any of this matter?"

Given the impact of the coercive style, you might assume it should never be applied. Our research, however, uncovered a few occasions when it worked masterfully. Take the case of a division president who was brought in to change the direction of a food company that was losing money. His first act was to have the executive conference room demolished. To him, the room—with its long marble table that looked like "the deck of the Starship *Enterprise*"—symbolized the tradition-bound formality that was paralyzing the company. The destruction of the room, and the subsequent move to a smaller, more informal setting, sent a message no one could miss, and the division's culture changed quickly in its wake.

That said, the coercive style should be used only with extreme caution and in the few situations when it is absolutely imperative, such as during a turnaround or when a hostile takeover is looming. In those cases, the coercive style can break failed business habits and shock people into new ways of working. It is always appropriate during a genuine emergency, like in the aftermath of an earthquake or a fire. And it can work with problem employees with whom all else has failed. But if a leader relies solely on this style or continues to use it once the emergency passes, the long-term impact of his insensitivity to the morale and feelings of those he leads will be ruinous.

The authoritative style

Tom was the vice president of marketing at a floundering national restaurant chain that specialized in pizza. Needless to say,

the company's poor performance troubled
the senior managers, but they were at a loss
for what to do. Every Monday, they met to
review recent sales, struggling to come up
with fixes. To Tom, the approach didn't
make sense. "We were always trying to figure out why our sales were down last week.
We had the whole company looking back-
ward instead of figuring out what we had to
do tomorrow."

Tom saw an opportunity to change people's way of thinking at an off-site strategy
meeting. There, the conversation began
with stale truisms: The company had to drive
up shareholder wealth and increase return
on assets. Tom believed those concepts
didn't have the power to inspire a restaurant

manager to be innovative or to do better than a good-enough job.

So Tom made a bold move. In the middle of a meeting, he made an impassioned plea for his colleagues to think from the customer's perspective. Customers want convenience, he said. The company was not in the restaurant business; it was in the business of distributing high-quality, convenient-to-get pizza. That notion—and nothing else—should drive everything the company did.

With his vibrant enthusiasm and clear vision—the hallmarks of the authoritative style—Tom filled a leadership vacuum at the company. Indeed, his concept became the core of the new mission statement. But this conceptual breakthrough was just the beginning. Tom made sure that the mission statement was built into the company's strategic planning process as the designated driver of growth. And he ensured that the vision was articulated so that local restaurant managers understood they were the key to the company's success and were free to find new ways to distribute pizza.

Changes came quickly. Within weeks, many local managers started guaranteeing fast, new delivery times. Even better, they started to act like entrepreneurs, finding ingenious locations to open new branches: kiosks on busy street corners and in bus and train stations, even from carts in airports and hotel lobbies.

Tom's success was no fluke. Our research indicates that of the six leadership styles, the authoritative one is most effective, driving up every aspect of climate. Take clarity. The authoritative leader is a visionary; he motivates people by making clear to them how their work fits into a larger vision for the organization. People who work for such leaders understand that what they do matters and why. Authoritative leadership also maximizes commitment to the organization's goals and strategy. By framing the individual tasks within a grand vision, the authoritative leader defines standards that revolve around that vision. When he gives performance feedback—whether positive or negative—the singular criterion is whether or not that performance furthers the vision. The standards for success are clear to all, as are the rewards. Finally, consider the style's impact on flexibility. An authoritative leader states the end but generally gives people plenty of leeway to devise their own means. Authoritative leaders give people the freedom to innovate, experiment, and take calculated risks.

Because of its positive impact, the authoritative style works well in almost any business situation. But it is particularly effective when a business is adrift. An authoritative leader charts a new course and sells his people on a fresh long-term vision.

The authoritative style, powerful though it may be, will not work in every situation.

The approach fails, for instance, when a leader is working with a team of experts or peers who are more experienced than he is; they may see the leader as pompous or out-of-touch. Another limitation: If a manager trying to be authoritative becomes overbearing, he can undermine the egalitarian spirit of an effective team. Yet even with such caveats, leaders would be wise to grab for the authoritative "club" more often than not. It may not guarantee a hole in one, but it certainly helps with the long drive.

The affiliative style

If the coercive leader demands, "Do what I say," and the authoritative urges, "Come with me," the affiliative leader says, "People come first." This leadership style revolves around people—its proponents value individuals and their emotions more than tasks and goals. The affiliative leader strives to keep employees happy and to create harmony among them. He manages by building strong emotional bonds and then reaping the benefits of such an approach, namely fierce loyalty. The style also has a markedly positive effect on communication. People who like one another a lot talk a lot. They share ideas; they share inspiration. And the style drives up flexibility; friends trust one another, allowing habitual innovation and risk taking. Flexibility also rises because the affiliative leader, like a parent who adjusts household rules for a maturing adolescent, doesn't impose unnecessary strictures on how employees get their work done. They give people the freedom to do their job in the way they think is most effective.

As for a sense of recognition and reward for work well done, the affiliative leader offers ample positive feedback. Such feedback has special potency in the workplace because it is all too rare: Outside of an annual review, most people usually get no feedback on their day-to-day efforts—or only negative feedback. That makes the affiliative leader's positive words all the more motivating. Finally, affiliative leaders are masters at building a sense of belonging. They are, for instance, likely to take their direct reports out for a meal or a drink, one-on-one, to see

how they're doing. They will bring in a cake
to celebrate a group accomplishment. They
are natural relationship builders.

Joe Torre, the heart and soul of the New
York Yankees, is a classic affiliative leader.
During the 1999 World Series, Torre tended
ably to the psyches of his players as they
endured the emotional pressure cooker of
a pennant race. All season long, he made a
special point to praise Scott Brosius, whose
father had died during the season, for stay-
ing committed even as he mourned. At the
celebration party after the team's final game,
Torre specifically sought out right fielder
Paul O'Neill. Although he had received
the news of his father's death that morning, O'Neill chose to play in the decisive

game—and he burst into tears the moment it ended. Torre made a point of acknowledging O'Neill's personal struggle, calling him a "warrior." Torre also used the spotlight of the victory celebration to praise two players whose return the following year was threatened by contract disputes. In doing so, he sent a clear message to the team and to the club's owner that he valued the players immensely—too much to lose them.

Along with ministering to the emotions of his people, an affiliative leader may also tend to his own emotions openly. The year Torre's brother was near death awaiting a heart transplant, he shared his worries with his players. He also spoke candidly with the team about his treatment for prostate cancer.

The affiliative style's generally positive impact makes it a good all-weather approach, but leaders should employ it particularly when trying to build team harmony, increase morale, improve communication, or repair broken trust. For instance, one executive in our study was hired to replace a ruthless team leader. The former leader had taken credit for his employees' work and had attempted to pit them against one another. His efforts ultimately failed, but the team he left behind was suspicious and weary. The new executive managed to mend the situation by unstintingly showing emotional honesty and rebuilding ties. Several months in, her leadership had created a renewed sense of commitment and energy.

Despite its benefits, the affiliative style should not be used alone. Its exclusive focus on praise can allow poor performance to go uncorrected; employees may perceive that mediocrity is tolerated. And because affiliative leaders rarely offer constructive advice on how to improve, employees must figure out how to do so on their own. When people need clear directives to navigate through complex challenges, the affiliative style leaves them rudderless. Indeed, if overly relied on, this style can actually steer a group to failure. Perhaps that is why many affiliative leaders, including Torre, use this style in close conjunction with the authoritative style. Authoritative leaders state a vision, set standards, and let people know how

their work is furthering the group's goals.
Alternate that with the caring, nurturing
approach of the affiliative leader, and you
have a potent combination.

The democratic style

Sister Mary ran a Catholic school system in a
large metropolitan area. One of the schools—
the only private school in an impoverished
neighborhood—had been losing money for
years, and the archdiocese could no longer
afford to keep it open. When Sister Mary
eventually got the order to shut it down,
she didn't just lock the doors. She called a
meeting of all the teachers and staff at the
school and explained to them the details of
the financial crisis—the first time anyone

working at the school had been included in the business side of the institution. She asked for their ideas on ways to keep the school open and on how to handle the closing, should it come to that. Sister Mary spent much of her time at the meeting just listening.

She did the same at later meetings for school parents and for the community and during a successive series of meetings for the school's teachers and staff. After two months of meetings, the consensus was clear: The school would have to close. A plan was made to transfer students to other schools in the Catholic system.

The final outcome was no different than if Sister Mary had gone ahead and closed the school the day she was told to. But by allowing the school's constituents to reach that decision collectively, Sister Mary received none of the backlash that would have accompanied such a move. People mourned the loss of the school, but they understood its inevitability. Virtually no one objected.

Compare that with the experiences of a priest in our research who headed another Catholic school. He, too, was told to shut it down. And he did—by fiat. The result was disastrous: Parents filed lawsuits, teachers and parents picketed, and local newspapers ran editorials attacking his decision. It took a year to resolve the disputes before he could finally go ahead and close the school.

Sister Mary exemplifies the democratic style in action—and its benefits. By spending time getting people's ideas and buy-in, a leader builds trust, respect, and commitment. By letting workers themselves have a say in decisions that affect their goals and how they do their work, the democratic leader drives up flexibility and responsibility. And by listening to employees' concerns, the democratic leader learns what to do to keep morale high. Finally, because they have a say in setting their goals and the standards for evaluating success, people operating in a democratic system tend to be very realistic about what can and cannot be accomplished.

However, the democratic style has its drawbacks, which is why its impact on climate is not as high as some of the other styles. One of its more exasperating consequences can be endless meetings where ideas are mulled over, consensus remains elusive, and the only visible result is scheduling more meetings. Some democratic leaders use the style to put off making crucial decisions, hoping that enough thrashing things out will eventually yield a blinding insight. In reality, their people end up feeling confused and leaderless. Such an approach can even escalate conflicts.

When does the style work best? This approach is ideal when a leader is himself uncertain about the best direction to take and needs ideas and guidance from able employees. And even if a leader has a strong vision, the democratic style works well to generate fresh ideas for executing that vision.

The democratic style, of course, makes much less sense when employees are not competent or informed enough to offer sound advice. And it almost goes without saying that building consensus is wrong-headed in times of crisis. Take the case of a CEO whose computer company was severely threatened by changes in the market. He always sought consensus about what to do. As competitors stole customers and customers' needs changed, he kept appointing committees to consider the situation. When the market made a sudden shift because of a new technology, the CEO froze in his tracks.

The board replaced him before he could appoint yet another task force to consider the situation. The new CEO, while occasionally democratic and affiliative, relied heavily on the authoritative style, especially in his first months.

The pacesetting style

Like the coercive style, the pacesetting style has its place in the leader's repertory, but it should be used sparingly. That's not what we expected to find. After all, the hallmarks of the pacesetting style sound admirable. The leader sets extremely high performance standards and exemplifies them himself. He is obsessive about doing things better and faster, and he asks the same of everyone around him.

He quickly pinpoints poor performers and demands more from them. If they don't rise to the occasion, he replaces them with people who can. You would think such an approach would improve results, but it doesn't.

In fact, the pacesetting style destroys climate. Many employees feel overwhelmed by the pacesetter's demands for excellence, and their morale drops. Guidelines for working may be clear in the leader's head, but she does not state them clearly; she expects people to know what to do and even thinks, "If I have to tell you, you're the wrong person for the job." Work becomes not a matter of doing one's best along a clear course so much as second-guessing what the leader wants. At the same time, people often feel that the pacesetter doesn't trust them to work in their own way or to take initiative. Flexibility and responsibility evaporate; work becomes so task focused and routinized it's boring.

As for rewards, the pacesetter either gives no feedback on how people are doing or jumps in to take over when he thinks they're lagging. And if the leader should leave, people feel directionless—they're so used to "the expert" setting the rules. Finally, commitment dwindles under the regime of a pacesetting leader because people have no sense of how their personal efforts fit into the big picture.

For an example of the pacesetting style, take the case of Sam, a biochemist in R&D

at a large pharmaceutical company. Sam's superb technical expertise made him an early star: He was the one everyone turned to when they needed help. Soon he was promoted to head of a team developing a new product. The other scientists on the team were as competent and self-motivated as Sam; his métier as team leader became offering himself as a model of how to do first-class scientific work under tremendous deadline pressure, pitching in when needed. His team completed its task in record time.

But then came a new assignment: Sam was put in charge of R&D for his entire division. As his tasks expanded and he had to articulate a vision, coordinate projects, delegate responsibility, and help develop others, Sam began to slip. Not trusting that his subordinates were as capable as he was, he became a micromanager, obsessed with details and taking over for others when their performance slackened. Instead of trusting them to improve with guidance and development, Sam found himself working nights and weekends after stepping in to take over for the head of a floundering research team. Finally, his own boss suggested, to his relief, that he return to his old job as head of a product development team.

Although Sam faltered, the pacesetting style isn't always a disaster. The approach works well when all employees are self-motivated, highly competent, and need little direction or coordination—for example, it can work for leaders of highly skilled and self-motivated professionals, like R&D groups or legal teams. And, given a talented team to lead, pacesetting does exactly that: gets work done on time or even ahead of schedule. Yet like any leadership style, pacesetting should never be used by itself.

The coaching style

A product unit at a global computer company had seen sales plummet from twice as much as its competitors to only half as much. So Lawrence, the president of the manufacturing division, decided to close the unit and reassign its people and products. Upon hearing the news, James, the head of the doomed unit, decided to go over his boss's head and plead his case to the CEO.

What did Lawrence do? Instead of blowing up at James, he sat down with his rebellious direct report and talked over not just the decision to close the division but also James's future. He explained to James how moving to another division would help him develop new skills. It would make him a better leader and teach him more about the company's business.

Lawrence acted more like a counselor than a traditional boss. He listened to James's concerns and hopes, and he shared his own. He said he believed James had grown stale in his current job; it was, after all, the only place he'd worked in the company. He predicted that James would blossom in a new role.

The conversation then took a practical turn. James had not yet had his meeting with the CEO—the one he had impetuously demanded when he heard of his division's closing. Knowing this—and also knowing that the CEO unwaveringly supported the closing—Lawrence took the time to coach James on how to present his case in that meeting. "You don't get an audience with the CEO very often," he noted. "Let's make sure you impress him with your thoughtfulness." He advised James not to plead his personal case but to focus on the business unit: "If he thinks you're in there for your own glory, he'll throw you out faster than you walked through the door." And he urged him to put his ideas in writing; the CEO always appreciated that.

Lawrence's reason for coaching instead of scolding? "James is a good guy, very talented and promising," the executive explained to us, "and I don't want this to derail his career. I want him to stay with the company, I want him to work out, I want him to learn, I want him to benefit and grow. Just because he screwed up doesn't mean he's terrible."

Lawrence's actions illustrate the coaching style par excellence. Coaching leaders help employees identify their unique strengths and weaknesses and tie them to their personal and career aspirations. They encourage employees to establish long-term development goals and help them conceptualize a plan for attaining them. They make agreements with their employees about their role and responsibilities in enacting development plans, and they give plentiful instruction and feedback. Coaching leaders excel at delegating; they give employees challenging assignments, even if that means the tasks won't be accomplished quickly. In other words, these leaders are willing to put up with short-term failure if it furthers long-term learning.

Of the six styles, our research found that the coaching style is used least often. Many leaders told us they don't have the time in this high-pressure economy for the slow and tedious work of teaching people and helping them grow. But after a first session, it takes little or no extra time. Leaders who ignore this style are passing up a powerful tool: Its impact on climate and performance are markedly positive.

Admittedly, there is a paradox in coaching's positive effect on business performance because coaching focuses primarily on personal development, not on immediate work-related tasks. Even so, coaching improves results. The reason: It requires constant dialogue, and that dialogue has a way of pushing up every driver of climate. Take flexibility. When an employee knows his boss watches him and cares about what he does, he feels free to experiment. After all, he's sure to get quick and constructive feedback. Similarly, the ongoing dialogue of coaching guarantees that people know what is expected of them and how their work fits into a larger vision or strategy. That affects responsibility and clarity. As for commitment, coaching helps there, too, because the style's implicit message is, "I believe in you, I'm investing in you, and I expect your best efforts." Employees very often rise to that challenge with their heart, mind, and soul.

The coaching style works well in many business situations, but it is perhaps most effective when people on the receiving end are "up for it." For instance, the coaching style works particularly well when employees are already aware of their weaknesses and would like to improve their performance.

Similarly, the style works well when employees realize how cultivating new abilities can help them advance. In short, it works best with employees who want to be coached.

By contrast, the coaching style makes little sense when employees, for whatever reason, are resistant to learning or changing their ways. And it flops if the leader lacks the expertise to help the employee along. The fact is, many managers are unfamiliar with or simply inept at coaching, particularly when it comes to giving ongoing performance feedback that motivates rather than creates fear or apathy. Some companies have realized the positive impact of the style and are trying to make it a core competence. At some companies, a significant portion of annual bonuses are tied to an executive's development of his or her direct reports. But many organizations have yet to take full advantage of this leadership style. Although the coaching style may not scream "bottom-line results," it delivers them.

LEADERS NEED MANY STYLES

Many studies, including this one, have shown that the more styles a leader exhibits, the better. Leaders who have mastered four or more—especially the authoritative, democratic, affiliative, and coaching styles—have the very best climate and business performance. And the most effective leaders switch flexibly among the leadership styles as needed. Although that may sound daunting, we witnessed it more often than you might guess, at both large corporations and tiny start-ups, by seasoned veterans who could explain exactly how and why they lead and by entrepreneurs who claim to lead by gut alone.

Such leaders don't mechanically match their style to fit a checklist of situations—they are far more fluid. They are exquisitely sensitive to the impact they are having on others and seamlessly adjust their style to get the best results. These are leaders, for example, who can read in the first minutes of conversation that a talented but underperforming employee has been demoralized by an unsympathetic, do-it-the-way-I-tell-you manager and needs to be inspired through a reminder of why her work matters. Or that leader might choose to reenergize the employee by asking her about her dreams and aspirations and finding ways to make her job more challenging. Or that initial conversation might signal that the employee needs an ultimatum: Improve or leave.

For an example of fluid leadership in action, consider Joan, the general manager of a major division at a global food and beverage company. Joan was appointed to her job while the division was in a deep crisis. It had not made its profit targets for six years; in the most recent year, it had missed by $50 million. Morale among the top management team was miserable;

mistrust and resentments were rampant. Joan's directive from above was clear: Turn the division around.

Joan did so with a nimbleness in switching among leadership styles that is rare. From the start, she realized she had a short window to demonstrate effective leadership and to establish rapport and trust. She also knew that she urgently needed to be informed about what was not working, so her first task was to listen to key people.

Her first week on the job she had lunch and dinner meetings with each member of the management team. Joan sought to get each person's understanding of the current situation. But her focus was not so much on learning how each person diagnosed the problem as on getting to know each manager as a person. Here Joan employed the affiliative style: She explored their lives, dreams, and aspirations.

She also stepped into the coaching role, looking for ways she could help the team members achieve what they wanted in their careers. For instance, one manager who had been getting feedback that he was a poor team player confided his worries to her. He thought he was a good team member, but he was plagued by persistent complaints. Recognizing that he was a talented executive and a valuable asset to the company, Joan made an agreement with him to point out (in private) when his actions undermined his goal of being seen as a team player.

She followed the one-on-one conversations with a three-day offsite meeting. Her goal here was team building, so that everyone would own whatever solution for the business problems emerged. Her initial stance at the off-site meeting was that of a democratic leader. She encouraged everyone to express freely their frustrations and complaints.

The next day, Joan had the group focus on solutions: Each person made three specific proposals about what needed to be done. As Joan clustered the suggestions, a natural consensus emerged about priorities for the business, such as cutting costs. As the group came up with specific action plans, Joan got the commitment and buy-in she sought.

With that vision in place, Joan shifted into the authoritative style, assigning account-ability for each follow-up step to specific executives and holding them responsible for their accomplishment. For example, the division had been dropping prices on products without increasing its volume. One obvious solution was to raise prices, but the previous VP of sales had dithered and had let the problem fester. The new VP of sales now had responsibility to adjust the price points to fix the problem.

Over the following months, Joan's main stance was authoritative. She continually articulated the group's new vision in a way that reminded each member of how his or her role was crucial to achieving these goals. And, especially during the first few weeks of the plan's implementation, Joan felt that the urgency of the business crisis justified an occasional shift into the coercive style should someone fail to meet his or her responsibility. As she put it, "I had to be brutal about this follow-up and make sure this stuff happened. It was going to take discipline and focus."

The results? Every aspect of climate improved. People were innovating. They were talking about the division's vision and crowing about their commitment to new, clear goals. The ultimate proof of Joan's fluid leadership style is written in black ink: After only seven months, her division exceeded its yearly profit target by $5 million.

EXPANDING YOUR REPERTORY

Few leaders, of course, have all six styles in their repertory, and even fewer know when and how to use them. In fact, as we have brought the findings of our research into many organizations, the most common responses have been, "But I have only two of those!" and, "I can't use all those styles. It wouldn't be natural."

Such feelings are understandable, and in some cases, the antidote is relatively simple. The leader can build a team with members who employ styles she lacks. Take the case of a VP for manufacturing. She successfully ran a global factory system largely by using the affiliative style. She was on the road constantly, meeting with plant managers, attending to their pressing concerns, and letting them know how much she cared about them personally. She left the division's strategy—extreme efficiency—to a trusted lieutenant with a keen understanding of technology, and she delegated its performance standards to a colleague who was adept at the authoritative approach. She also had a pacesetter on her team who always visited the plants with her.

An alternative approach, and one I would recommend more, is for leaders to expand their own style repertories. To do so, leaders must first understand which emotional intelligence competencies underlie the leadership styles they are lacking. They can then work assiduously to increase their quotient of them.

For instance, an affiliative leader has strengths in three emotional intelligence competencies: in empathy, in building relationships, and in communication. Empathy—sensing how people are feeling in the moment—allows the affiliative leader to respond to employees in a way that is highly congruent with that person's emotions, thus building rapport. The affiliative leader also displays a natural ease in forming new relationships, getting to know someone as a person, and cultivating a bond. Finally, the outstanding affiliative leader has mastered the art of interpersonal communication, particularly in saying just the right thing or making the apt symbolic gesture at just the right moment.

So if you are primarily a pacesetting leader who wants to be able to use the affiliative style more often, you would need to improve your level of empathy and, perhaps, your skills at building relationships or communicating effectively. As another example, an authoritative leader who wants to add the democratic style to his repertory might need to work on the capabilities of collaboration and communication. Such advice about adding capabilities may seem simplistic—"Go change yourself"—but enhancing emotional intelligence is entirely possible with practice. (For more on how to improve emotional intelligence, see the sidebar "Growing Your Emotional Intelligence.")

MORE SCIENCE, LESS ART

Like parenthood, leadership will never be an exact science. But neither should it be a complete mystery to those who practice it. In recent years, research has helped parents understand the genetic, psychological, and behavioral components that affect their "job performance." With our new research, leaders, too, can get a clearer picture of what it takes to lead effectively. And perhaps as important, they can see how they can make that happen.

The business environment is continually changing, and a leader must respond in kind. Hour to hour, day to day, week to week, executives must play their leadership styles like a pro—using the right one at just the right time and in the right measure. The pay-off is in the results.

NOTE

Daniel Goleman consults with Hay/McBer on leadership development.

Getting Molecular: The Impact of Leadership Styles on Drivers of Climate

Our research investigated how each leadership style affected the six drivers of climate, or working atmosphere. The figures below show the correlation between each leadership style and each aspect of climate. So, for instance, if we look at the climate driver of flexibility, we see that the coercive style has a –.28 correlation while the democratic style has a .28 correlation, equally strong in the opposite direction. Focusing on the authoritative leadership style, we find that it has a .54 correlation with rewards—strongly positive—and a .21 correlation with responsibility—positive, but not as strong. In other words, the style's correlation with rewards was more than twice that with responsibility.

According to the data, the authoritative leadership style has the most positive effect on climate, but three others—affiliative, democratic, and coaching—follow close behind. That said, the research indicates that no style should be relied on exclusively, and all have at least short-term uses.

	Coercive	Authoritative	Affiliative	Democratic	Pacesetting	Coaching
Flexibility	−.28	.32	.27	.28	−.07	.17
Responsibility	−.37	.21	.16	.23	.04	.08
Standards	.02	.38	.31	.22	−.27	.39
Rewards	−.18	.54	.48	.42	−.29	.43
Clarity	−.11	.44	.37	.35	−.28	.38
Commitment	−.13	.35	.34	.26	−.20	.27
Overall impact on climate	−.26	.54	.46	.43	−.25	.42

The Six Leadership Styles at a Glance

Our research found that leaders use six styles, each springing from different components of emotional intelligence. Here is a summary of the styles, their origin, when they work best, and their impact on an organization's climate and thus its performance.

	Coercive	Authoritative
The leader's modus operandi	Demands immediate compliance	Mobilizes people toward a vision
The style in a phrase	"Do what I tell you."	"Come with me."
Underlying emotional intelligence competencies	Drive to achieve, initiative, self-control	Self-confidence, empathy, change catalyst
When the style works best	In a crisis, to kick-start a turnaround, or with problem employees	When changes require a new vision, or when a clear direction is needed
Overall impact on climate	Negative	Most strongly positive

	Affiliative	Democratic
The leader's modus operandi	Creates harmony and builds emotional bonds	Forges consensus through participation
The style in a phrase	"People come first."	"What do you think?"
Underlying emotional intelligence competencies	Empathy, building relationships, communication	Collaboration, team leadership, communication
When the style works best	To heal rifts in a team or to motivate people during stressful circumstances	To build buy-in or consensus, or to get input from valuable employees
Overall impact on climate	Positive	Positive

(continued)

{ 179 }

	Pacesetting	Coaching
The leader's modus operandi	Sets high standards for performance	Develops people for the future
The style in a phrase	"Do as I do, now."	"Try this."
Underlying emotional intelligence competencies	Conscientiousness, drive to achieve, initiative	Developing others, empathy, self-awareness
When the style works best	To get quick results from a highly motivated and competent team	To help an employee improve performance or develop long-term strengths
Overall impact on climate	Negative	Positive

Emotional Intelligence: A Primer

Emotional intelligence—the ability to manage ourselves and our relationships effectively—consists of four fundamental capabilities: self-awareness, self-management, social awareness, and social skill. Each capability, in turn, is composed of specific sets of competencies. Below is a list of the capabilities and their corresponding traits.

Self-Awareness

- *Emotional self-awareness:* the ability to read and understand your emotions as well as recognize their impact on work performance, relationships, and the like.

- *Accurate self-assessment:* a realistic evaluation of your strengths and limitations.

- *Self-confidence:* a strong and positive sense of self-worth.

Self-Management

- *Self-control:* the ability to keep disruptive emotions and impulses under control.

- *Trustworthiness:* a consistent display of honesty and integrity.

- *Conscientiousness:* the ability to manage yourself and your responsibilities.

- *Adaptability:* skill at adjusting to changing situations and overcoming obstacles.

- *Achievement orientation:* the drive to meet an internal standard of excellence.

- *Initiative:* a readiness to seize opportunities.

Social Awareness

- *Empathy:* skill at sensing other people's emotions, understanding their perspective, and taking an active interest in their concerns.

- *Organizational awareness:* the ability to read the currents of organizational life, build decision networks, and navigate politics.

- *Service orientation:* the ability to recognize and meet customers' needs.

Social Skill

- *Visionary leadership:* the ability to take charge and inspire with a compelling vision.

- *Influence:* the ability to wield a range of persuasive tactics.

- *Developing others:* the propensity to bolster the abilities of others through feedback and guidance.

- *Communication:* skill at listening and at sending clear, convincing, and well-tuned messages.

- *Change catalyst:* proficiency in initiating new ideas and leading people in a new direction.

- *Conflict management:* the ability to de-escalate disagreements and orchestrate resolutions.

- *Building bonds:* proficiency at cultivating and maintaining a web of relationships.

- *Teamwork and collaboration:* competence at promoting cooperation and building teams.

Growing Your Emotional Intelligence

Unlike IQ, which is largely genetic—it changes little from childhood—the skills of emotional intelligence can be learned at any age. It's not easy, however. Growing your emotional intelligence takes practice and commitment. But the payoffs are well worth the investment.

Consider the case of a marketing director for a division of a global food company. Jack, as I'll call him, was a classic pacesetter: high-energy, always striving to find better ways to get things done, and too eager to step in and take over when, say, someone seemed about to miss a deadline. Worse, Jack was prone to pounce on anyone who didn't seem to meet his standards, flying off the handle if a person merely deviated from completing a job in the order Jack thought best.

Jack's leadership style had a predictably disastrous impact on climate and business results. After two years of stagnant performance, Jack's boss suggested he seek out a coach. Jack wasn't pleased but, realizing his own job was on the line, he complied.

The coach, an expert in teaching people how to increase their emotional intelligence, began with a 360-degree evaluation of Jack. A diagnosis from multiple viewpoints is essential in improving emotional intelligence because those who need the most help usually have blind spots. In fact, our research found that top-performing leaders overestimate their strengths on, at most, one emotional intelligence ability, whereas poor performers overrate themselves on four or more. Jack was not that far off, but he did rate himself more glowingly than his direct reports, who gave him especially low grades on emotional self-control and empathy.

Initially, Jack had some trouble accepting the feedback data. But when his coach showed him how those weaknesses were tied to his inability to display leadership styles dependent on those competencies—especially the authoritative, affiliative, and coaching styles—Jack realized he had to improve if he wanted to advance in the company. Making such a connection is essential. The reason: Improving emotional intelligence isn't done in a weekend or during a seminar—it takes diligent practice on the job, over several months. If people do not see the value of the change, they will not make that effort.

Once Jack zeroed in on areas for improvement and committed himself to making the effort, he and his coach worked up a plan to turn his day-to-day job into a learning laboratory. For instance, Jack discovered he was empathetic when things were calm, but in a crisis, he tuned out others. This tendency hampered his ability to listen to what people were telling him in the very moments he most needed to do so. Jack's plan required him to focus on his behavior during tough situations. As soon as he felt himself tensing up, his job was to immediately step back, let the other person speak, and then ask clarifying questions. The point was to not act judgmental or hostile under pressure.

The change didn't come easily, but with practice Jack learned to defuse his flare-ups by entering into a dialogue instead of launching a harangue. Although he didn't always agree with them, at least he gave people a chance to make their case. At the same time, Jack also practiced giving his direct reports more positive feedback and reminding them of how their work contributed to the group's mission. And he restrained himself from micromanaging them.

Jack met with his coach every week or two to review his progress and get advice on specific problems. For instance, occasionally Jack would find himself falling back on his old pacesetting tactics—cutting people off, jumping in to take over, and blowing up in a rage. Almost immediately, he would regret it. So he and his coach dissected those relapses to figure out what triggered the old ways and what to do the next time a similar moment arose. Such "relapse prevention" measures inoculate people against future lapses or just giving up. Over a six-month period, Jack made real improvement. His own records showed he had reduced the number of flare-ups from one or more a day at the beginning to just one or two a month. The climate had improved sharply, and the division's numbers were starting to creep upward.

Why does improving an emotional intelligence competence take months rather than days? Because the emotional centers of the brain, not just the neocortex, are involved. The neocortex, the thinking brain that learns technical skills and purely cognitive abilities, gains knowledge very quickly, but the emotional brain does not. To master a new behavior, the emotional centers need repetition and practice. Improving your emotional intelligence, then, is akin to changing your habits. Brain circuits that carry leadership habits have to unlearn the old ones and replace them with the new. The more often a behavioral sequence is repeated, the stronger the underlying brain circuits become. At some point, the new neural pathways become the brain's default option. When that happened, Jack was able to go through the paces of leadership effortlessly, using styles that worked for him—and the whole company.

Article Summary

Idea in Brief

Many managers mistakenly assume that leadership style is a function of personality rather than strategic choice. Instead of choosing the one style that suits their temperament, they should ask which style best addresses the demands of a particular situation.

Research has shown that the most successful leaders have strengths in the following emotional intelligence competencies: **self-awareness**, **self-regulation**, **motivation**, **empathy**, and

social skill. There are six basic styles of leadership; each makes use of the key components of emotional intelligence in different combinations. The best leaders don't know just one style of leadership—they're skilled at several, and have the flexibility to switch between styles as the circumstances dictate.

INDEX

achievement motivation,
    34–40, 183
adaptability, 183
affiliative leaders, 119,
    136–143, 172, 177, 179
age, emotional
    intelligence and,
    12–13
ambiguity, 33
amygdala, 66, 78, 80
anxiety, 67–68
attention
  cognitive control of,
    71–75
  creativity and, 91–92

excellence and, 95–96
focusing, viii–ix,
    63–64, 111–112
  inward, 64, 65–75, 112
  outward, 64, 75–94, 112
  selective, 91–92, 100
  strengthening, 95,
    98–100
authentic selves, 68–71
authoritative leaders, 119,
    130–136, 173, 177, 178
automated social
    hierarchy detection, 86
awareness. *See also* self-
    awareness

awareness (*continued*)
  expanding your,
    101–103
  open, 69–71, 92,
    101–103
  organizational, 183–184
  social, 183–184
  systems, 92–94
  triad of, ix, 64, 112

Baron-Cohen, Simon, 93
belonging, 138–139
big-picture thinking, 9
biological impulses,
  26–27
body language, 46
Boyatzis, Richard, 103
Brosius, Scott, 139

candor, 21–22, 25–26
change, 29–31, 33
change catalyst, 185
charisma, 34

clarity, 123, 128, 134,
  160, 177
climate
  affiliative leaders and,
    137–138
  authoritative
    leaders and,
    134–135
  coaching leaders and,
    159–160
  coercive leaders and,
    127–128
  definition of, 123
  democratic leaders and,
    146–147
  drivers of, 176–177
  leadership styles and,
    122–125, 176–177,
    178–180
  pacesetting leaders and,
    150–151
coaching, 47–48, 116, 177,
  187–193
coaching leaders,
  119, 154–162, 180

Index

coercive leaders, 119,
125–130, 177, 178
cognitive abilities, 4, 7,
9, 55, 186
cognitive control, 71–75,
104–106
cognitive empathy, 76,
77–78, 83, 110
collaboration, 173, 185
commitment
to common purpose,
123
to the organization, 39,
40, 134, 151, 160
common purpose,
commitment to, 123
communication, 137, 172,
173, 185
compassion fatigue, 81
competency models, 6–8
competition, 29–30
conflict management, 185
conscientiousness, 182
consensus, 43–44, 147, 148

Consortium for Research
on Emotional
Intelligence in
Organizations, 14
creative insight, 90–92
cross-cultural
dialogue, 45–47

Davidson, Richard, 84
decision making
empathy and, 41
gut feelings and,
66–68
self-awareness and,
20–21
democratic leaders, 119,
143–149, 177, 179
detachment, 107–108
development
of emotional
intelligence, 12–18
of others, 154–162, 184
diligence, 95

Index

distractions
  filtering, 63
  resisting, 74

effective leadership, 3–5,
  115–125
emergencies, 130
emotional empathy,
  76, 78–79,
  107–108, 110
emotional intelligence
  components of, viii,
    57–60
  definition of, 181
  development of, 12–18,
    56, 186–193
  empathy component of,
    40–49, 58, 60
  evaluating, 6–11
  genetic component
    of, 12
  leadership and, 4–6,
    197–198

leadership styles
  and, 171–173,
    178–180
  motivation component
    of, 34–40, 57, 60
  performance and, 9–11,
    59, 120–125
  self-awareness
    component of,
    19–26, 57, 60, 65–71,
    181–182
  self-regulation
    component of,
    26–34, 57, 60,
    182–183
  social awareness
    component of, 183–184
  social skill
    component of,
    49–55, 58, 60,
    184–185
emotional pleas, 52
emotional self-
  awareness, 181

Index

emotions, 26–27, 50

empathic concern, 76, 79–82

empathy, viii, 12, 40–49, 58, 60

  affiliative leaders and, 172

  cognitive, 76, 77–78, 83, 110

  controlling, 109–110

  deficit, 93

  definition of, 183

  emotional, 76, 78–79, 107–108, 110

  expressing, 55

  importance of, 43–48

  learning, 107–108

  training to increase, 15–18

Eriksen Flanker Task, 104

etiquette, 83

executive function, 71

exploitation, 88–89

exploration, 88–89

external rewards, 34–35

failure

  admitting, 23

  learning from, 38–39

fairness, 28

feedback

  increasing emotional intelligence through, 13, 17

  performance, 123, 134–135

  positive, 138

  360-degree, 187–188

fiery temperament, 33–34

flexibility, 123, 127, 135, 137–138, 146, 151, 159–160

fluid leadership, 162–169

Index

focus
  of attention, viii–ix,
    63–64, 111–112
  inward, ix, 64,
    65–75, 112
  on others, ix, 64,
    75–87, 112
  outward, ix, 64,
    75–94, 112
  on strategy, 88–90
  strengthening, 95,
    98–100
focused leaders,
  94–97
friendliness, 49–50

gamma waves, 90–91
Gates, Bill, 88
George, Bill, 70–71
globalization, 45–47
goals
  concentrating on
    future, 74

positive, 102–103
  self-awareness and,
    20–21
gut feelings, 66–68

heartbeat, awareness
  of, 66
hierarchy, 85–87
hippocampus, 78, 84
hiring process, 22–23
humor, sense of, 23
hypothalamus, 78

impulses, 26–28,
  31–32
influence, 184
information
  overload, 96
initiative, 183
inner voice, 65
innovation, 90–92
inquisitiveness, 77

insula, 65–66
integrity, 31–33, 57
intelligence, 4, 9
interpersonal
    communication, 172
intuition, 66–68
inward focus, ix, 64,
    65–75, 112
IQ, 4, 9, 55, 186

judgment calls, 25–26

leaders
  actions of, 115–116
  emotional intelligence
    of, 4–6, 55–56,
    59–60, 197–198
  focused, 94–97
leadership
  effective, 3–5, 115–125
  experts, 116–117
  fluid, 162–169

measuring impact of,
    120–125
research on, 174–175
skills, training in, 13
of teams, 43–45, 51
visionary, 184
leadership styles, ix–x, 4,
    117–120, 178–180
  affiliative, 119,
    136–143, 172, 177, 179
  authoritative, 119,
    130–136, 173,
    177, 178
  climate and, 122–125,
    127–128, 134–135,
    137–138, 146–147,
    150–151, 159–160,
    176–177, 178–180
  coaching, 119, 154–162,
    177, 180
  coercive, 119, 125–130,
    177, 178
  democratic, 119,
    143–149, 177, 179

emotional intelligence
and, 178–180
learning new, 170–173
pacesetting, 119,
149–154, 177, 180
switching between,
119–120, 162–169, 198
learning
brain and, 13–14
emotional intelligence,
12–18, 56, 186–193
empathy, 107–108
limbic system, 13, 14–15
Litwin, George, 123
long-term vision, 9
loyalty, 137

marshmallow test, 73–75
maturity, 13
McClelland, David,
10–11, 120–121, 123
meditation, 98–100, 106
mentoring, 47–48.
See also coaching

mergers, 29, 41–43
mindfulness, 106
Mischel, Walter, 72–73, 74
mission clarity, 123, 128
moral judgments,
81–82
motivation, viii, 34–40,
51, 52, 55, 57, 60
Musical Chairs, 105, 106

neocortex, 13–14, 192
networks, social, 50,
84–85
neural networks, 91,
109–110, 192–193
neuroscience, 63
neurotransmitters, 13

O'Neill, Paul, 139–140
open awareness, 69–71,
92, 101–103
optimism, 37–38, 40, 51,
102–103

orbitofrontal cortex, 78
organizational
    awareness, 183–184
organizational
    commitment, 39, 40,
    134, 151, 160
organizational hierarchy,
    85–87
others
  development of,
    154–162, 184
  focus on, ix, 64,
    75–87, 112
outward focus, ix, 64,
    75–94, 112
oxytocin, 80

pacesetting leaders, 119,
    149–154, 177, 180
passion, 35, 52
performance
  climate and, 124–125
  coaching style and,
    159–160

emotional intelligence
    and, 9–11, 59, 120–125
  personal capabilities
    driving, 7–11
  raising bar of, 36–37,
    39–40
performance feedback,
    123, 134–135
performance reviews, 23,
    36–37
persuasion, 51–52
pessimism, 102
positive feedback, 138
positive thinking,
    37–38, 40, 51,
    102–103
prefrontal cortex, 71, 80,
    84, 109–110
progress tracking, 37
psychic attrition, 85
psychologists, 6–8

rapport building, 50, 172
recognition, 138

reflection, 33
relationship building,
    52–54, 82–87, 139,
    172, 185
relationship management,
    49–51, 55
responsibility, 123, 127,
    146, 151, 160
rewards system, 123, 128,
    135, 138, 151
Riess, Helen, 107–108

selective attention,
    91–92, 100
self-assessment, 182
self-awareness
    authenticity and, 68–71
    cognitive empathy and,
        77–78
    as component
        of emotional
        intelligence, viii,
        19–26, 57, 181–182
    definition of, 60

emotional, 181
    inward focus and, 65–71
    self-assessment and, 182
self-confidence,
    23–24, 182
self-control, 71–75, 182
self-depreciation, 23
self-gratification, 74
self-management,
    182–183
self-regulation, 26–34,
    57, 60, 182–183
self-restraint, 104–106
self-revelation, 70–71
service orientation, 184
Simon, Herbert, 96
Singer, Tania, 78–79
social and emotional
    learning (SEL)
    method, 105–106
social awareness, 183–184
social context, 83–84
social hierarchy, 85–87
social networks, 50,
    84–85

social sensitivity, 82–85
social skill, viii, 49–55, 58, 60, 184–185
somatic markers, 66–68
standards, 123, 134, 142
star performers, 9–10
status quo, 35
strategy, focusing on, 88–90
Stringer, Richard, 123
systems awareness, 92–94

talent retention, 47–48
team harmony, 141
team leadership, 43–45, 51
teamwork, 185
technical skills, 4, 7, 9, 55
Tenacity (game), 99–100
thoughtfulness, 33
360-degree feedback, 187–188

threshold capabilities, 4–5
Torre, Joe, 139–140, 142
training
  emotional intelligence, 13–18
  leadership, 13
True North groups, 70–71
trust, 28, 141, 146, 165
trustworthiness, 57, 182

values, 123
vigilance, 91
vision, 134, 135, 142
visionaries, 87–88
visionary leadership, 184

willpower, 71–75
wimpiness, 25
working environment, 123

ABOUT THE AUTHOR

Daniel Goleman is a codeveloper of GolemanEI coaching and training programs and a codirector of the Consortium for Research on Emotional Intelligence in Organizations at Rutgers University, coauthor of *Primal Leadership: Leading with Emotional Intelligence* (Harvard Business Review Press, 2013), and author of *The Brain and Emotional Intelligence: New Insights* and *Leadership: The Power of Emotional Intelligence: Selected Writings*

(More Than Sound, 2011). His latest book is *A Force for Good: The Dalai Lama's Vision for Our World* (Bantam, 2015).

The most important management ideas all in one place.

We hope you enjoyed this book from *Harvard Business Review*. For the best ideas HBR has to offer turn to HBR's 10 Must Reads Boxed Set. From books on leadership and strategy to managing yourself and others, this 6-book collection delivers articles on the most essential business topics to help you succeed.

HBR's 10 Must Reads Series

The definitive collection of ideas and best practices on our most sought-after topics from the best minds in business.

- Change Management
- Collaboration
- Communication
- Emotional Intelligence
- Innovation
- Leadership
- Making Smart Decisions

- Managing Across Cultures
- Managing People
- Managing Yourself
- Strategic Marketing
- Strategy
- Teams
- The Essentials

hbr.org/mustreads

Buy for your team, clients, or event.
Visit hbr.org/bulksales for quantity discount rates.